LEST WE

A CONCISE COM╷ ╷O THE FIRST WORLD WAR

STEPHEN LIDDELL

ISBN-10: 1500490113

ISBN-13: 978-1500490119

DEDICATION

This book is dedicated to the brave men and women who both fought and died in The Great War.

At the going down of the sun and in the morning,
We will remember them

In particular to those relations of mine that I never got to meet including Private Ernest Heard S/N 24500 of The Loyal North Lancashire Regiment who died in Mesopotamia on 25th January 1917 and who is buried in Amara, Iraq. Serjent Reuel Dunn S/N 6396 of the Royal Flying Corp who was shot down by the Red Baron on 2nd April 1917 and is buried in the Cabaret-Rouge British Cemetery, Souchez, France. George Hardy Liddell S/N 315010, 12th/13th Bn., Northumberland Fusiliers who died on 22 August 1918 and is buried in the Connaught Cemetery, Thiepval, France.

Their Name Liveth Forevermore.

CONTENTS

ACKNOWLEDGMENTS

Kind acknowledgements are made to Endeavour Press for their wonderful cover image and their assistance in creating a better history book.

Thanks also to the various institutions who have helped me with various queries and copyright issues and to my wonderful wife Emilia for her undying support during the creation of this work.

Finally, grateful appreciation is given to Tonja Bliss whose expertise was enormously helpful in the creation of this paperback edition.

1   INTRODUCTION

The coming four years see the 100th anniversary of The Great War, now more commonly known as World War One in which 16 million people died, and a further 20 million were wounded. There will be increased publicity and interests to events which there are sadly no longer any first-hand witnesses.

Many books will no doubt be released that will go into great and often overwhelming detail of every aspect of World War 1. If that is what you're looking for, then this book probably shouldn't be the first that you pick up, though perhaps it could be the second. Instead, this book is written in a simple and easy to understand manner for those interested in this Great War that shook the world and re-shaped it and which is the foundation of the modern world and modern Britain.

Instead of looking at the minutiae of tactics and manoeuvres throughout this long and awful war, this book instead focuses on the key events and themes that you will either have heard about, or no doubt will hear about in the near future.

Broken into 27 easy to read sections which will give you all you need to know about this most important of historical events as well as photos of some of the key figures and easy to understand maps of the more important themes in the book.

This book covers all of the main events of the war and explains them in as simple a way as possible, whether it's The Somme, Lawrence of Arabia, The Red Baron or the

Christmas Truce and football match. This book will help you learn about the trenches, the impact of war at home and all around the world as well as the many repercussions that we are still living with today both good and bad.

Whether you know little about WW1 and want to learn the basics or if you simply want a comprehensive guide that you can read in a few hours then this book is for you and will help you with all the WW1 events going on and act as an introduction for those who might to want to read something more involved later.

The author is a young qualified historian and writer who has visited WW1 and WW2 battlefields in the U.K., Europe and Middle-East and wants to bring this important war to the attention of the many people who don't want to tackle heavy and overly complicated history books.

.

2   THE ROAD TO WAR

How and why World War One came about is one of the most complicated aspects of history with different historians placing lesser or greater emphasis on numerous interrelated events. There was a time when everyone at school learned that it all came down to the assassination of the Austrian Archduke Franz Ferdinand, but that is a terribly simplistic explanation.

To find the truths behind The Great War, it is necessary to look at Europe in the late 19th Century. Europe was a land dominated by empires, by the far the most powerful was that of the British, which had limited holdings in Europe itself but was overwhelmingly the most important of The Great Powers and controlled a vast global empire by way of the Royal Navy. France was perhaps the second greatest global power and though in no way comparable to the British Empire it was in all other respects still a major imperial power.

Eastern and South-eastern Europe was dominated by the increasingly aged and impotent Austro-Hungarian Empire centred on Vienna and The Ottoman Empire with its capital in Istanbul. Such was the weakness of these empires that their long subjugated peoples were striving and fighting with much success for independence which resulted in creating fledging states in modern day Greece, Romania, Bulgaria and Serbia.

The modern state of Germany which we know today had for

centuries been a loose confederation of states which were only unified in the second half of the 19th Century by the militarily powerful Prussians. Due to its late formation as a unified nation-state Germany did not have any imperial holdings and it wanted them badly. Germany saw itself as a natural equal to the Great Powers and particularly looked up to and wanted to surpass the glory of the British Empire and so it began creating for itself a disparate set of Imperial colonies in parts of Africa and the Far-East. However the continued expansion of the German Empire was very much dependant on the good will of the British who naturally did not want to see their supremacy challenged, least of all by an aggressive and competing European state.

To make matters worse, Germany was governed by the Kaiser who treated his country as his personal fiefdom and well able to over-rule its toothless parliament. Kaiser Willhelm II came to power on 15th June 1888, a grandson of the British Queen Victoria. His mother had problems at his birth leading to the young Willhelm suffering from a withered arm and he was ridiculed for his slight disability at a time when it was essential for a monarch to be seen to be healthy, fit and virile. Perhaps it was due to this that Willhelm had a tendency to overcompensate with his aggressive and militaristic actions almost as if he had an inferiority complex. In fact even as the Kaiser on his trips to the United Kingdom, he perceived himself to be not treated as an equal with the British royal family and nobility whilst back in Germany he was widely seen as being more British than German which no doubt riled him greatly.

Once Queen Victoria and his mother had died, both in 1901, the Kaiser no longer felt he had any special obligations towards Britain and instead started to plot to at best, displace Britain from her primacy or at least shear away the colonies from London. It was a controversial policy even within Germany with many believing that they had left it too late to build an empire and even those who agreed with the Kaiser's ambition believing that notions of nationalism and democracy would make this imperial endeavour untenable not just to subject people overseas put to the German politicians and people at home.

In order to have any chance of success, it was necessary for Germany to embark on a massive militarization programme. Germany teamed up with its allies to the south and east, the Austro-Hungarian Empire sometimes known as the Hapsburgs and also with Italy. This created the Triple Alliance whilst on the 8th April 1904 Britain and France solidified their previous decades of peace with the Entente Cordiale. In 1907 a similar agreement was reached with Russia leading to what became known as the Triple Entente. This effectively made the three empires allies against their common enemy Germany. It also ended Britain's policy of splendid isolation in Europe and having now seen off the global ambitions of France and Russia, it was time to safeguard the Empire from the antagonistic Prussians.

Another important factor in the road to war was the 1839 Treaty of London which saw Europe and most importantly Great Britain guarantee the sovereignty and independence of Belgium. Everyone in Europe knew about this treaty but Germany didn't think Britain would invoke it should Belgian sovereignty be impinged upon. Similarly Britain didn't expressly state that it would go to war merely for the sake of tiny Belgium. Nevertheless there was a widespread feeling in Europe that war was looming and that it was largely inevitable. All that was needed was for a flashpoint to flare up and in Europe there were many flashpoints.

There was a rampant nationalism in the Balkans where groups were fighting for recognition, political reform and independence. The Archduke who ruled over the Austro-Hungarian Empire was extremely elderly and wasn't really up to the stresses of running of a modern state. Much hope was pinned on his son, Archduke Franz Ferdinand who had aspirations for political reform to create a family of equal Austrian states in a similar manner to the United States of America. On the 28th June 1914, Archduke Franz Ferdinand went with his wife Sophie, the Duchess of Hohenberg went to Sarajevo. He was not a popular figure in Sarajevo as there were many in the city who hoped to join with their Slavic cousins in Serbia however as his visit was to amongst other things open a museum and a hospital it was perhaps naively hoped that it wouldn't be too dangerous.

There had already been previous assassination attempts on Austrian officials by members of the Black Hand group and they were now planning to attack the Archduke on his official visit.

Having arrived in Sarajevo by train, the royal couple ventured into the city in an open top car. Six terrorists lay in wait amongst the crowds all with the aim of killing the Archduke when his car drew near. The first member lost his nerve as the car drove past whilst the second threw a bomb but due to its 10 second delay fuse, it exploded late hitting the 4th car in the convoy. It's occupants and bystanders in the street were severely injured but the royal couple were unscathed. The 19 year old bomber was named Nedeljko Čabrinović and immediately after the attack he swallowed a cyanide capsule and jumped into the river but the cyanide was old and didn't work rendering him merely unwell. It being midsummer, the river was just a few inches deep and he was immediately captured.

Understandably unnerved by the attack, the convoy sped through the city so fast that the remaining terrorists were unable to mount an attack. It was decided that the Archduke would travel to the hospital to visit the survivors of the earlier attack by driving along the Appel Quay rather than through the city centre but his driver took a wrong turn and drove past Moritz Schiller's café where another member of the Black Hand group called Gavrilo Princip by chance just happened to be standing in the doorway ready for a drink believing that all chance of killing the Archduke had passed. Gavrilo Princip was caught totally by surprise when the car of the Archduke went unexpectedly passed him and cursing his luck went inside the café.

The Archduke driver realised he had taken a wrong turn and reversed his car. In the confusion and panic of the earlier events, the driver stalled the car just outside the café. Gavrilo Princip seized the unexpected opportunity and stepped out to just 5 feet from the car firing twice. Seeing her husband under attack, Duchess Sophia dived to cover his body and was hit in the abdomen whilst the Archduke was hit in the neck. Franz leaned over his wife crying. He was still alive when witnesses arrived to render aid. His dying words to Sophia were, 'Don't die darling, live for our children.' The Archduke died within minutes and his beloved wife Sophie died en-route to hospital. Gavrilo Princip and his colleagues were rounded up and he died in prison in 1918.

The initial view not just in London but in Paris and other

capitals was that this was just the latest in a long series of unrest in the Balkans and certainly not worthy of any war. Indeed, public reaction in Austria itself was minimal and life went on as before though in Sarajevo the Austrian authorities clamped down on Serbian communities that were violently persecuted.

There was a month of complex political and diplomatic manoeuvrings with Austria under intense behind the scenes pressure from Germany and issuing Serbia ten demands in an ultimatum. Germany wanted a war because it was stronger militarily than Russia and France and indeed a decision to go to war had already been taken before the assassination. Germany also felt that Britain would never go to war due to a Balkans crisis even if Russia and France were drawn into it and to that end Germany did everything they could to start an Austro-Serbian war without being seen in any way to encourage it.

A looming election in Serbia meant that it was difficult for the Serbian government to appear weak to Austria but even so accepted 8 out of the 10 points in the ultimatum with Britain repeatedly offering to mediate to ensure peace.

Nevertheless with Germany offering Austria any support required and literally demanding military action, at 11am on July 28th 1914, Austro-Hungary declared war on Serbia. Russia, unwilling to see their Slavic brothers once again under the yoke of an empire, partially mobilised its military on July 29th. Germany mobilised its military on July 30th and Russia enacted a full mobilisation immediately in response.

Austria was hoping for a short minor war against Serbia and on 12th August mounted an invasion of Serbia but to its surprise was strongly repulsed with high casualties at the Battles of Cer and Kolubara. Not only was there to be no quick victory for the Austrians but even worse they was forced to maintain a strong force on the Serbian front which it vitally needed against Russia.

Germany expected an attack from both France and Russia and as such put into place a modified version of the Schlieffen Plan which would send its army sweeping in an arc through Belgium and surrounding the French army on the French/German border to put the French out of the war before things really got going. The French though did not want to allow any misunderstanding and ordered its army to stand back several miles from the border with Germany.

Germany requested free travel through Belgium which the Belgian government refused to authorise and so Germany invaded anyway. On the 3rd August under Prime Minister Herbert Asquith, the British government issued an ultimatum to Germany that it withdraw from Belgium. The ultimatum passed at midnight without any heed from Germany and so a message was telegrammed from Admiralty House in London to all Royal Navy forces to commence hostilities against Germany.

Shortly later PM Asquith addressed a packed House of Commons:

"We have made a request to the German Government that we shall have a satisfactory assurance as to the Belgium neutrality before midnight tonight. The German reply to our request was unsatisfactory." The Prime Minister continued that an extremely unsatisfactory reply was received in which Germany stated they were attacking to avoid a French invasion of Germany itself.

"Owing to the summary rejection by the German Government of the request made by His Majesty's Government for assurances that the neutrality of Belgium would be respected, His Majesty's Ambassador in Berlin has received his passport, and His Majesty's Government has declared to the German Government that a state of war exists between Great Britain and Germany as from 11pm on August 4th."

The British Empire, Europe though not yet the world was now at war and as the Foreign Secretary Sir Edward Grey allegedly put it "The lamps are going out all over Europe, we shall not see them lit again in our life-time".

3   OVER BY CHRISTMAS

Following the British Declaration of War on 4th August 1914, the government made great efforts to mobilise the army and indeed recruit new volunteers from the general population into the army as quickly as possible. Without the benefit of hindsight, many on both sides thought that the looming war would be 'Over by Christmas'.

The German Kaiser insisted to his men that they would be home before the leaves fall from the trees and that there was a general opinion amongst the German forces that they would be putting their feet up in Paris in about six weeks time.

Similar views were commonplace in Russia where most officers considered a six-week war would be all that would be taken before they reached Berlin and those few who thought it might take several months were considered unpatriotic pessimists.

This view was very similar to that in Britain with indeed the notable exception of Lord Kitchener, who expected the war to last at least three years and possibly more with the requirement of 1 million men needed. Whilst more informed people may have had their doubts that the war was going to be a short one, it wasn't in the interest of the government or military to say otherwise. In fact, the whole thing took on something of a party atmosphere with groups of men joining up as they didn't want to miss out on the fun. The usually brief wars with relatively few casualties of the Victorian Age were still fresh in everyone's memories, and indeed, many of the Generals of WW1 spent much of their time in Victorian wars but unlike the Victorian Bush wars or the earlier Napoleonic and other historic campaigns, this war was going to be different and fought against modern European Armies with 20th century weaponry even if the Generals themselves were from the 19th Century.

The government and media whipped up a storm of encouraging propaganda for young men to volunteer and fight the war before it was too late. Whether the British Expeditionary Force or the armies of the other European nations would have been so enthusiastic if they had known they were would be marching into oblivion in a war that was to last four years, it is highly doubtful. People of all nations of this time were much more patriotic and unquestioning of authority. If their betters said that they should do something then more often and not they did so and without question.

Nationalism played a terrible part in this rush to war. In Russia, it allowed the Tsar to mobilise support as a way to save his country and indeed his skin, the Austro-Hungarians to regain control over Eastern Europe whilst others used it to win freedom for their nations. Germany simply wanted to gain an Empire like the French and British that Kaiser Wilhelm II thought was his due. The French fought to save their country but with the British it was slightly different. Great Britain wasn't directly involved in the conflict and already had the largest Empire in history. It was the world policeman and when Germany invaded tiny neutral Belgium it was time to put the German upstarts in their place, It offered a generation of enthusiastic young men the chance to serve God, King and country and when such glories awaited, who wouldn't want to join their friends for a bit of fun and glory?

4   THE PALS BATTALIONS

The British Army had been and still is one that was very small considering its worldwide scope of actions. Unlike other nations which had large standing armies, for the British Army success depended not on its size but on its training, discipline, tactics and applied technology as well as a strong Royal Navy. There is a well-known quote attributed to the Duke of Wellington that states that British soldiers weren't braver than anyone else but that their discipline allowed them to be brave for just 5 minutes longer than their opponents and often that was all it took. This approach meant that when The Great War fired up, that Great Britain had a woefully small army and the generals of the time believed that due to the sheer scope of the war, a vast recruitment drive would be needed.

Long before other nations, the British Army had been a professional force whereas, in others, many boys and men were conscripted and forced to undergo a period of military service; indeed some places in the world still do that today. Even WW1 did not change the values in Britain until several years of fighting and so to recruit enough men and Lord Kitchener, who was then Secretary of State for War along with General Sir Henry Rawlinson came up with the idea that men would be more likely to join-up if they did so with their pals and colleagues. The plan was tested in the City of London when 1,600 men enlisted into what was colloquially known as the Stockbroker Battalion in August 1914.

Just a few days later 1,500 more men from Liverpool formed

another battalion at the behest of the Earl of Derby, who proclaimed "This should be a battalion of pals, a battalion in which friends from the same office will fight shoulder to shoulder for the honour of Britain and the credit of Liverpool."

Lord Kitchener saw the success of these first two battalions and took the idea across the country and within a month over 50 towns had formed their own battalions with the cities contributing several at a time. It is from this time that the famous recruiting poster first came out with Lord Kitchener pointing his finger with the subtitle of "Your Country Needs You".

Battalions were formed from almost every imaginable source of men including public schools, factories, offices and there were even two formed consisting solely of footballers with Hearts from Edinburgh losing 7 of their first team players in the war alone.

The first two years of the war saw 1,000 battalions formed with over half of these being Pals Battalions and their casualties were terrible, to say the least, especially during The Somme. For example, The Accrington Pals along with Pals Battalions drawn from the Yorkshire cities of Leeds, Sheffield, Bradford and the town of Barnsley were ordered to attack Serre on 1st July 1916, and it took until February until Serre was taken. In just the first 20 minutes of the attack out of the 700 Accrington Pals, 235 were killed and 350 wounded. A walk now along the old quiet lanes around Serre and you can see the cemeteries, some large, some containing just a handful of soldiers buried almost where they fell.

Of course, as the Pals Battalions were formed out of local

communities, it meant that when battles had high casualties, certain communities suffered disproportionately high losses with some villages, towns and districts losing almost all their men.

The unprecedented high mortality rate in the British Army meant that the policy of Conscription was enacted in January 1916 as by that time anyone who had wanted to volunteer had already done so and many had sadly had died too. By 1917, most Pals Battalions had become so under strength that they were amalgamated into other units.

5   THE RACE TO THE SEA

Long before the war started the Germans had created the Schlieffen Plan and it was a modified version of this plan that they carried out when they invaded Belgium and marched through tiny Luxembourg. France had readied its armies which were waiting on the Belgian border. Whilst in Belgium the German Army committed great atrocities and many villages were burnt to the ground in what became known as 'The Rape of Belgium'.

The Battle of the Frontiers saw a number of engagements in the Mons area with the French Fifth Army being all but destroyed though it did achieve a 24-hour delay in the German advance. The Allies including a small but increasing British Expeditionary Force were compelled to retreat until the Germans were just 43 miles from Paris. The Germans were finally halted at the First Battle of the Marne, which took place on 6-12th September 1914.

The German troops retreated and began to dig in defensive positions, and so the western front began to take on its static form that was to plague the war for much of the next four years. As the Germans dug in, so did the Allies and so began 'The Race to the Sea'. It wasn't so much a race by armies to reach the sea but competing efforts by the British and Germans to outflank each other. It started around the 17th September and continued until 19th October 1914 when the Belgians reached the North Sea. The period was noted for several small-scale battles but nothing in any way decisive. A similar process happened further south between predominantly French and German forces until the Western Front formed all the way from the North Sea to the Swiss border.

There were a number of battles where the Germans tried to push their way through, and the Allies tried to both repulse them and push them back, and in places, the French were on the brink of collapse until reinforced by the increasing number of British soldiers. The final attempt in the early phase of the war by the Germans to push through near the coast was the First Battle of Ypres on the 19th-22nd October 1914 after which the German area commander Erich Von Falkenhayn concluded that it was an impossible task. Unfortunately, by then the casualty rate was already soaring with 116,000 dead Germans, and 800,000 casualties and the French losing 454,000 men whilst the British had 89,964 killed. Incredibly over 50% of the Belgian army had been lost.

6   THE CHRISTMAS TRUCE

The accounts of the Christmas Truce in 1914 between the British and German armies are some of the most legendary and heart-warming in modern history. It was a chance for the ordinary men of both sides to meet their opponents and find out that they were pretty much the same as their supposed enemies.

There wasn't any official truce along the whole length of the Western Front but rather a number of more local truces. There had already been a small number of informal moments of quiet where burial details were allowed out into No Mans Land to collect bodies and at least on one occasion following a heavy rain storm, both British and German troops climbed out of the trenches to escape mud without anyone opening fire.

General De Gaulle of France was extremely unhappy with bored French soldiers getting acquainted with the Germans and having occasional cross-trench visits so when Pope Benedict XV asked that "that the guns may fall silent at least upon the night the angels sang" it was no surprise that his pleas fell on deaf ears.

However, the feeling of the men on the ground who actually had to endure the awful conditions and had no real gripes with their opponents was very different and with the front line trenches often being just a few feet apart it was very easy to contact the other side. In the week leading up to Christmas, there had been a number of attempts by soldiers of each side to make contact with the enemy. On occasion, both sides would sing Christmas carols with 'Silent Night' being the preferred choice by the Jerrys whilst the Tommies favoured 'Oh Come All Ye Faithful' and sometimes even joint services were held.

Around Ypres, Germans began decorating their trenches with candles and a British soldier who was a hairdresser in civilian life actually trimmed the hair of some Germans, and there are many similar incredible events detailed in letters sent back home.

There were even a number of football matches played in No-Mans Land between British soldiers and the Germans, sometimes they had balls with them but if not then items such as ration tins could be used.

One of the reasons that there were several football matches was because the men from both sides couldn't easily communicate with each other, so the men had to find a way to spend their time in a friendly manner. There was an exchange of gifts with sometimes different alcoholic beverages being swapped or more commonly Bully Beef for German cigars.

The generals on both sides took a very dim view at the events and for the Christmas of 1915, there were very specific orders put in place to ensure that it should not re-occur including deliberately shelling and raiding opposition trenches on Christmas Day itself. Despite this, a small number of truces were formed though not as numerous or long-lasting as the previous year where some had ran on for several days. In one area a football was produced with a mass free-for-all on both sides, but the men were recalled back, and orders given the firing must resume by the afternoon, and the soldiers were threatened with disciplinary action and in some other places with being shot.

It was much harder for truces to occur in the later years as both sides had such ingrained animosities but the Germans did make offers to their British counterparts. However the savage toll suffered at The Somme, and the use of poison gas had understandably changed the attitudes of the Tommies. Troops were also rotated to different areas of the front to stop them becoming overly familiar with the Germans across the narrow battlefield.

There were similar but smaller scaled truces between Germans and French and Belgian troops in 1914 and also a local one between Austria and Russia.

Much is made of how World War One marks the introduction of a new type of war, a total war. Be that as it may, it was also the death of the old type of chivalry which used to be a common part of warfare, especially involving British and other northern European states. The Christmas Truce is perhaps the last great example of this happening in ground warfare though it persisted a little while longer in aerial combat.

7 LIFE IN THE TRENCHES

Though only a minority of soldiers were actually in the trenches at any one time, the trenches of the Western Front are nevertheless the first things that come to mind when many of us think of WW1. What was life in the trenches like?

The first trenches were nothing more than hastily dug ditches that were not intended to be anything other than temporary shelters to get men out of the way of enemy gunfire. As time progressed, though, trenches expanded exponentially both in their coverage and complexity.

Shelters and command posts began to be built underground with wooden supports that though kept the rain and bullets out, did little to protect against lucky artillery shell or mortar strike. Later on, quarters and command posts began to be boosted by the use of concrete and with electricity and telephone cables and some places provided a modicum of comfort for the lucky few not on the front line itself.

Trenches rarely ran more than a few dozen feet before changing direction in a zigzag fashion otherwise, a well-placed artillery shell would see the shockwave push for hundreds of yards along the trench, killing or injuring everyone in its path. A whole network of support trenches stretched back from the front line, often a dozen miles back from the front used for communications, reserve troops and bringing in supplies. To make it feel a bit like home, the soldiers would often name their trenches after famous streets in London or their home cities.

Soldiers would be rotated to spend time at the front, and the length and frequency of their placements there would depend on how busy a sector they happened to be posted in. Typically a soldier might expect in a year to spend some 70 days on the front line, with another 30 in nearby support trenches. A further 120 might be spent in reserve. Only 70 days might be spent at rest. The amount of leave varied, with perhaps two weeks being granted during the year.

The distance between the front line of the Allies and that of the Germans varied from just a few feet to several hundred. The area in between was known as No-Mans Land as no one owned it and anyone who tried to enter it would quite probably end up dead. Miles of barbed fences and barbs would cover No-Mans Land and often there were land mines, unexploded ordinance and shell craters that were so deep that the water that collected in them could quickly drown an unsuspecting man or horse.

Death was a constant companion to those serving on the front line even when no raid or attack was launched or defended against. In busy sectors, the constant shellfire directed by the enemy brought random death to those both standing in a trench and those sheltering in a dug-out and many men were buried alive when dug-out shelters were hit by artillery shelling.

British soldier Harry Drinkwater kept a journal, something he had to do covertly as it was highly illegal. Even just a handful of his experiences in the trenches highlight just how awful it was for the common soldier in the trenches.

Monday, December 20

The trenches are in a terrible condition — anything up to 4ft deep in mud and water. We're plastered in mud up to our faces.

Our food – cold bacon, bread and jam – is slung together in a sack that hangs from the dripping dugout roof. Consequently, we eat and drink mud.

Tuesday, December 21

Heavy bombardment at about 11 am. Heard a fearful crash. The next dugout to ours blown to blazes, and our physical drill instructor Sergeant Horton with it.

I helped dig him out. But before we could get him anywhere, he'd departed this life – our first experience of death. I'm tired out, sick of everything.

Friday, December 31

Back on the firing line, and nearly up to our waists in mud. We've found a new diversion — at dusk, we put a small piece of cheese on the end of a bayonet, wait for a rat to have a nibble, and then pull the trigger.

Wednesday, March 8

Snowed all night. Had a hard job to keep awake. One or two fellows – of whom I was one – were found to be fast asleep at the end of their sentry. We'd gone to sleep standing up –

and the relief man was also asleep.

Under military law, this is a crime punishable by execution. So, as a preventative, we've arranged between ourselves that each sentry along the trench will fire his rifle at intervals.

At dusk, I put my head over the top to have a look around and stopped a bullet on the side of my steel hat. The vibration made my head ache.

Friday, May 19

The Germans forestalled us this morning by about three hours. After three months of hard work, our K14 mine, timed to go up at 8am, was blown in by the Germans at 4.30am.

There was a terrific explosion. The ground for yards around was lifted skywards, leaving a huge crater in the ground.

Captain Edwards, our company captain, crept out over my parapet to investigate the damage and was met by a fusillade of bullets. He stopped one through the shoulder and one in the head.

The moment after he was hit, an engineer sprang on to the parapet and, crawling on his stomach, dragged him back.

It's worth noting that the German sentry who shot Edwards could also have shot his rescuer. If he refrained from humane motives, he was a sportsman.

It was common for newly arrived soldiers were often

tempted to peer over the parapet of the trench to see what was happening on the other side of No Mans Land. However such curiosity would often be met with a well-aimed bullet from one of the many snipers who spent their time just waiting for such an opportunity to get themselves an easy kill.

Some estimations are that up to a third of casualties on the Western Front occurred in the trenches and whilst bullets and shells obviously played their part, just as notorious were the disease and conditions that the men had to live in. There were millions of rats in the trenches with brown rats in particular hated and feared by the Tommies as they would gorge themselves on human remains, often growing massively in size to almost resemble cats. Sometimes the rats would even gnaw on soldiers who were sleeping, or even just stationary and men were always worried their eyes would be eaten away. Soldiers would try to exterminate them by shooting, stabbing and clubbing them to death but it was a hopeless task as each pair of rats could produce up to 900 young rats each year with all the disease and infection that they bring.

Though neither side managed to get a grip on the rat problem, they did have one tiny redeeming fact, and that was that many men believed that rats could sense the approach of heavy shelling as they disappeared seconds before the shells hit which gave some men a slight warning of what was to come.

Other pest problems were nits, only avoided by shaving hair, and lice which bred like wildfire in the filthy uniforms the men wore causing a constant and painful itch. Lice even caused Trench Fever whilst the squeamish also had to deal with never ending waves of frogs, slugs and beetles.

For the first two years of the war, a major problem was that of Trench Foot. This was caused by a fungal infection brought on by having feet in constant cold, wet and muddy conditions. Untreated it could turn gangrenous and possibly require amputating. As life in the trench slowly improved as the war went on, it became less of an issue in the second half of the war.

Aside from the constant and ever-present shelling and the potential for an unexpected raid, the daily routine of life in the trenches was rather predictable with each day beginning with the morning 'stand-to'. An hour before dawn everyone was roused from slumber by the company orderly officer and sergeant and ordered to climb up on the fire step to guard against a dawn raid by the enemy with their bayonets fixed to their rifles.

This policy of 'stand-to' was adopted by both sides, and despite the knowledge that each side prepared itself for raids or attacks timed at dawn many were still actually carried out at this time. The men referred to this period as the 'morning hate' and both sides would often relieve the tension of the early hours with machine gun fire, shelling and small arms fire.

When the stand-to was completed, then the men would be expected to clean their rifle and equipment followed by an officer's inspection. Sometimes rum could be drank before breakfast was served; often there were local truces to allow breakfast to be eaten in relative peace and safety. However, they could stop at a moments notice as soon as any senior officer learned what was going on.

Following breakfast and their inspection, the men would be put to the task of completing their assigned daily duties such as draining trenches, repairing and replacing duckboards and refilling sandbag or preparing latrines.

After all the daily tasks were done, men could attend to their personal matters such as corresponding with their family, preparing and eating meals and snatching a little sleep for a few minutes at a time. As in the morning, dusk brought another stand-to to guard against any surprise attack as the light worsened. Once the trenches were secure for another night, then men would be sent back to collect water and rations from the back lines.

New men would be brought forward for night-time sentry duty on the fire step, and they would stay there for around two hours. They couldn't stay for much longer as the extreme tiredness of the men would make them prone to falling asleep at their post which rendered the line prone to attack but even more worryingly for the unfortunate men involved, sleeping on duty was, of course, punishable by death by firing squad.

From time to time, both sides would send out small patrols into No Mans Land to add new defences or repair existing barbed wire while others would sneak up to listening posts to try and overhear enemy chatter. Should patrols from both sides ever met in No Mans Land then they would have to instantly decide whether run away or engage in brutal hand to hand combat.

Patrols would often be sent out into No Mans Land. Some men would be tasked with repairing or adding barbed wire to the front line. Others, however, would go out to assigned listening posts, hoping to pick up valuable information from the enemy lines.

Sometimes enemy patrols would meet in No Man's Land. They were then faced with the option of hurrying on their separate ways or else engaging in hand to hand fighting. Firing their weapons was usually not a possibility as it would attract machine gun fire that would be deadly to everyone in the vicinity, friend and foe alike.

One aspect of life in the trenches that can't be emphasised enough is that of the awful smell that surrounded them. There were dead and rotting corpses of men and animals all over the place, hundreds of thousands in some of the key battle sites such as The Somme and many of those that had been buried were buried in hurried and shallow graves.

The latrines would often overflow and their stink would overpower even the smell of the men who had not bathed for weeks or even months and their wet feet and boots were known to be particularly repugnant smelling. If all that wasn't enough there was often the smell of rotting sandbags, lingering small quantities of poison gas, stagnant mud and water, smoke from cigarettes and gunfire as well as food being cooked. It says much that the men based there became used to it whilst it thoroughly overcame first-time visitors to the front.

8   WAR LITERATURE AND POETRY

It can often seem impossible to imagine anything constructive coming out of WW1, but one of the few undeniable plus points from the war was that of its poetry. Though British wars since the Crimean had allowed war correspondents to cover the ups and downs of military campaigns, the First World War took things to a new level. Additionally, better communications and levels of literacy meant that the ordinary Tommy was able to exchange letters with those back home.

There wasn't a great deal to do when off-duty and posted in the trenches asides from trying to keep dry, fed and sheltering from enemy gunfire. To counter their boredom and to try and have a break from their routine many would keep diaries or even try their hand at creative writing, especially poetry.

Many poems became internationally famous even if sadly in many cases the writers themselves had already been killed in action. WW1 poetry is a fascinating and rewarding area of literature and is a way of connecting directly with the misery, suffering and general life experiences from all those years ago.

To those who haven't read WW1 poetry, it is easy to lump it all together, but this would be doing a great injustice to all of the writers. The WW1 poets each have their own experiences and outlook on life and their differing views come through in their writing and by reading a number of them, not only do we gain an insight into their mindset but also gain a more rounded picture of what these soldiers had to endure during the war itself.

For many, if they have only had a fleeting experience of WW1 poets then it is likely that they read Rupert Brooke. Perhaps one of the most well-known poems in modern English literature is his work 'The Soldier'. It is sad, mournful and beautiful and still learned today by school children. Rupert Chawner Brooke was born on 3rd August 1887, the second of three children to a well-off family. He was educated at two Independent schools, travelled across Europe and studied at Cambridge University. It was here that his handsome good looks and with writing talent to match that he became acquainted with the Bloomsbury group of writers.

Suffering from a nervous breakdown in 1912 following a breakdown in his relationship with his partner, Ka Cox, he recuperated by way of travelling across North America whilst writing for the Westminster Gazette before slowly meandering across the South Pacific.

Rupert Brooke entered the war in October 1914 by joining the Royal Navy taking part in the Antwerp expedition and later seeing action in the Mediterranean where he was due to take part in the 1915 Gallipoli landings but sadly was bitten by a mosquito whose bite turned septic and he died at 4.46pm on 23rd April 1915 and his friend William Denis Browne was with him at the time writing "...I sat with Rupert. At 4 o'clock he became weaker, and at 4.46 he died, with the sun shining all round his cabin, and the cool sea-breeze blowing through the door and the shaded windows. No one could have wished for a quieter or a calmer end than in that lovely bay, shielded by the mountains and fragrant with sage and thyme."

Rupert Brooke was buried on the Greek island of Skyros in a small olive grove where his grave remains well tended today. He is also remembered in Poets Corner in Westminster Abbey.

Rupert Brooke was already on the way to prominence even before his untimely death as two of his sonnets were published in the Times Literary Supplement on 11th March 1915 and 'The Soldier' was read from the pulpit of St. Pauls Cathedral on Easter Sunday of that year. Following his death, however, his fame spread across the empire, and he remains amongst the most read WW1 poets around the world.

The Soldier

If I should die, think only this of me:
That there's some corner of a foreign field
That is for ever England. There shall be
In that rich earth a richer dust concealed;
A dust whom England bore, shaped, made aware,
Gave, once, her flowers to love, her ways to roam,
A body of England's, breathing English air,
Washed by the rivers, blest by suns of home.

And think, this heart, all evil shed away,
A pulse in the eternal mind, no less
Gives somewhere back the thoughts by England given;
Her sights and sounds; dreams happy as her day;
And laughter, learnt of friends; and gentleness,
In hearts at peace, under an English heaven.

by Rupert Brooke

Perhaps the leading WW1 poet is Wilfred Owen. He is much

adored particularly by historians as his approach is quite different to the approach taken by Rupert Brooke. Wilfred Own was born the first of four children in 1893 to a family of modest means in Shropshire. His childhood was marked by his father having to repeatedly move home to find work, and he was a devout Christian. He had already begun writing poetry in 1903 and was heavily influenced by The Bible and the romantic poets and John Keats in particular.

Wilfred Own gained entry to London University but not with First Class Honours, which was the only way his to gain a scholarship which his working class family needed to finance his studies. Instead, he was compelled to attend Reading College where he studied, taking some free classes and assisting with the local church in return for free lodgings.

Wilfred Owen was an English school teacher working in Continental Europe. He visited a hospital for the injured which immediately compelled him to return to Britain and enlist in the Army where he joined Artists Rifles Officers Training Corps. His positive outlook changed during the war as he endured a number of traumatic experiences suffering concussion and being blown sky high by a mortar which left him isolated and alone laying amongst dead comrades for several days in a crater. Diagnosed with shellshock in March 1917 he was sent to recuperate in a hospital in Edinburgh where he became friends with Siegfried Sassoon whose own poetry and character would drastically change Wilfred Owens' outlook on life.

Following time spent on regimental duties in the U.K. during which he wrote many of his most famous works, Wilfred Owen was declared fit for duty and returned to the war in August 1918. On 1st October, he led a storming of a number of German positions near Joncourt by the Second Manchesters. Just a week before the end of the war, Wilfred Owen was sadly killed by German machine gunners whilst crossing the Sambre Canal. Such was the speed of communication that his parents were sitting in their home in Shrewsbury at 11 am on 11th November 1918 happy that the war was over and their son had survived when there was a knock on the door. It was a telegram informing them their son was dead.

In July 1919 he was posthumously awarded the Military Cross with a citation:

For conspicuous gallantry and devotion to duty in the attack on the Fonsomme Line on October 1st/2nd, 1918. On the company commander becoming a casualty, he assumed command and showed fine leadership and resisted a heavy counter-attack. He personally manipulated a captured enemy machine gun from an isolated position and inflicted considerable losses on the enemy. Throughout he behaved most gallantly.

ANTHEM FOR DOOMED YOUTH

What passing-bells for these who die as cattle?
 Only the monstrous anger of the guns.
 Only the stuttering rifles' rapid rattle
Can patter out their hasty orisons.
No mockeries for them; no prayers nor bells,
Nor any voice of mourning save the choirs,—
The shrill, demented choirs of wailing shells;
And bugles calling for them from sad shires.

What candles may be held to speed them all?

Not in the hands of boys, but in their eyes
Shall shine the holy glimmers of goodbyes.
The pallor of girls' brows shall be their pall;
Their flowers the tenderness of patient minds,
And each slow dusk a drawing-down of blinds.

by Wilfred Owen   The author kindly acknowledges that this poem was taken from Wilfred Owen: The War Poems (Chatto & Windus, 1994), editor, Jon Stallworthy.

Edward Thomas was born into a Welsh family in Lambeth, London on 3rd March 1917. He was educated at Battersea Grammar School and latterly at Oxford during which he married. Edward Thomas was born to write and became a prolific book reviewer, frequently penning 15 reviews per week. He went on to become a literary critic though he didn't serious indulge in writing poetry until 1914.

Unlike other WW1 poets, Edward Thomas was married with children at the time of WW1 and considerably older too at the age of 37 when he decided he had to fight for King and Country. He could have used his age to stay out of the war but instead joined the Artists Rifles in July 1915 and rose through the ranks until he became 2nd Lieutenant in the Royal Garrison Artillery.   Soon after arriving in France he saw action in Arras but died on Easter Monday, 9th April 1917. Tragically he wasn't killed by enemy action but by the concussive blast waves of one of the very last artillery shells fired as he emerged to light his pipe.

Edward Thomas is buried at Agny in the Military Cemetery and is again commemorated at Poets Corner in Westminster Abbey. He had a deep love for the natural countryside and many of his poems reflect this.

In Memoriam (Easter, 1915)

The flowers left thick at nightfall in the wood
This Eastertide call into mind the men,
Now far from home, who, with their sweethearts, should
Have gathered them and will do never again.

By Edward Thomas

Perhaps the most famous poem of all to come out of the First World War is that of 'In Flanders Field' which was written by John McCrae in 1915. He was born on 30th November 1872 in Ontario, Canada, the Grandson of Scottish settlers and studied Guelph Collegiate Vocational Institute but due to problems with his asthma his undergraduate studies at Toronto University were put on hold for a year. He was a capable student of English, mathematics and medicine and gave private tuition to help pay his way through medical school.

His career as a physician was a notable one, becoming the resident pathologist at Montreal General Hospital and later worked at the Royal Victoria Hospital in Montreal before coming to England where he studied and became a member of the Royal College of Physicians.

As well as taking increasingly senior positions in the Canadian health-care system, he also served with the artillery in the Second Boer War. He then became a professor, teacher and published author but when Great Britain declared war on Germany, Canada as a Dominion found itself at war too and John McCrae was appointed as a Field Surgeon with the Canadian Artillery at the Second Battle of Ypres in 1915. It was here that his friend Lt. Alexis Helmer was killed and as his friend and doctor, John McCrae was overcome with emotion after his burial that he wrote the following poem.

In Flanders Field (May 1915)

In Flanders fields the poppies blow
Between the crosses, row on row,
That mark our place; and in the sky
The larks, still bravely singing, fly
Scarce heard amid the guns below.

We are the Dead. Short days ago
We lived, felt dawn, saw sunset glow,
Loved and were loved, and now we lie
In Flanders fields.

Take up our quarrel with the foe:
To you from failing hands we throw
The torch; be yours to hold it high.
If ye break faith with us who die
We shall not sleep, though poppies grow
In Flanders fields.

The poem soon appeared in Punch magazine and McCrae was re-posted to create a new Canadian Field Hospital. Aware of his fast-growing fame, he found it quietly amusing. Sadly, John McCrae died from complications brought on by pneumonia on 28th January 1918 and is buried in the Wimereux Cemetery. His famous poem became part of the inspiration for the use of the poppy as a symbol of remembrance and was used to encourage enlistment in the USA in the last year of WW1. It remains perhaps the most quoted poem on the annual Armistice Remembrance services.

Of course, The Great War was a world war and it wasn't just the English speaking soldiers that took to writing their thoughts down on paper. France, Italy and many other nations produced nationally famous poets. Perhaps though none of them quite approach the beauty of the English language texts or are quite as beloved by their readers. Naturally just as each Allied poet drew upon his own experiences and emotions then unavoidably poets of the Axis powers had a different point of view. This goes particularly for German poets whose culture and philosophy were increasingly shaped by the view of inevitable defeat. A visit to any German WW1 cemetery quickly shows the more brutalist and less reverential approach to their soldiers in stark contrast to the genteel, romantic like gardens of the Commonwealth graveyards.

More German poets seem to have survived the war than British poets or perhaps we just remember ours more but one notable German poet who fought in the war was August Stramm. Born on 29th July 1874 he grew up to work in the German Post Office and then performed the mandatory years conscription in the German Army. After visiting the United States on numerous occasions, August Stramm settled down no doubt for what he hoped would be a peaceful life in Berlin and began the life of a play-write.

He was already a reservist in the German Army and attained the highest rank possible by civilians, that of Captain. He was called to active service in August 1914 and was sent to the Western Front and in January 1915 was awarded The Iron Cross (Second Class) for his brave actions there. He was then transferred to the Eastern Front where first as Company Leader and then Battalion Commander but was later killed in fierce hand to hand combat at Horodec in what is today Belarus.

The poetry of August Stromm was already gaining prominence before his death and further publications were made after the end of the war. His work is typical of one of the first proponents of Expressionism which originated in Germany and sought to present poems from a subjective point of view to invoke angst and emotion rather than describe physical reality. Different as the writing style is, it is nevertheless evocative in its own way.

Guard Duty

A star frightens the steeple cross
a horse gasps smoke
iron clanks drowsily
mists spread
fears
staring shivering
shivering
cajoling
whispering
You!

9 VERDUN

The Battle of Verdun is less well known in Britain and some other places than those famous battles primarily involving the English-speaking Allies but it holds a tragic place in French history and rightly so. Additionally, the Battle of The Somme can not be fully appreciated without understanding the actions at Verdun, which preceded it.

Famously, Marshal Petain rallied his beleaguered nation with his slogan "Ils ne passeront pas" which translates as "They Shall Not Pass" and this typifies the sheer bloody-minded determination that the French displayed in this epic bleak and bloody battle.

Verdun was for many years the strongest French point along its defences with Germany and there were several forts safeguarding the town. It did however sit in a French salient, surrounded on three sides by German territory and peculiarly after the war started many of its defences were removed which encouraged the Germans into attacking what had been a secure defensive position since the times of the Romans.

The Battle of Verdun was fought from 21st February until 18th December 1916 and saw 50 divisions (roughly 1.25 million Germans) attack 85 French divisions (approximately 1.14 million French) with the French suffering an estimated 315-542,000 casualties including 156,000 dead whilst Germany saw up to 434,000 casualties with 143,000 dead. Unlike the wide front at The Somme, the French and German front lines at Verdun were no more than 15 miles long. With 32 million shells fired, some estimates state that in many areas of the battlefield 10 artillery shells fell on each square centimetre of soil.

The initial German attack was repeatedly delayed by snow but when it came, it was deadly. The German plan was to capture the Meuse Heights, which overlooked Verdun but only with the intention of provoking a French counterattack to push the Germans back. Then with their reserves brought forward would they would be an easy target for the concentrated German artillery in the area whilst German troops stayed relatively safe in pre-planned and pre-prepared strong defensive positions. French Military Intelligence had warned that such an attack was coming but they were ignored by the French High Command. The low levels of troops stationed there were taken by surprise by the massive artillery attack on February 21st 1916 which was simply to soften up French resistance for the infantry attack that was bound to follow just a few hours later.

When the infantry advance came, the Germans overcame stiff but always inadequate French resistance and on February 25th the Germans occupied Fort Douaumont. Marshal Petain rushed French re-enforcements to the area and they were thrown into the battle with orders to repel the Germans at all costs.

Despite enormous casualties, the French managed to stem the German advance and when Petain ordered that bloody counter-attacks be made the French forces eventually found themselves under the withering artillery attack that the Germans had long planned but it seemed to have little of the impact which the Germans had hoped for. Nevertheless, for the unfortunate foot soldiers on the receiving end of the barrage, it must have seemed like the end of the world.

In his journal a French officer, Lieutenant Henri Desagneaux, wrote: "Numb and dazed, without saying a word and with our hearts pounding, we await the shell that will destroy us... There's death everywhere. At our feet, the wounded groan in a pool of blood. Two of them, more seriously hit, are breathing their last. One, a machine-gunner, has been blinded, with one eye hanging out of its socket and the other torn out: in addition he has lost a leg. The second has no face, an arm blown off and a horrible wound in the stomach. Moaning and suffering atrociously, one begs me: 'Lieutenant, don't let me die.'"

Though the earlier battles in the first two years of war had in some ways been worse for the French Army, Verdun brought about a new level of mechanised sophistication to the war. Put simply, there was almost no end in the way that a French soldier might at any moment be killed. Raking machine gunfire, heavy artillery bombardment and a new modern terror from Germany, the flame thrower. Countless men were simply obliterated by exploding shells or buried alive under mounds of soil thrown up by explosives. Some were hit by shrapnel that cut them to pieces whilst vast numbers were left physically entirely unscathed though covered by the bloody body parts of their friends wondering mutely why they survived at all. Many of these lucky ones suffered extreme shell-shock and combat fatigue syndrome where if they were lucky they would spend the rest of their likely short lives trapped in their own unique mental hell or at worst be shot at dawn for supposed cowardice.

March saw the Germans widen their scope of the attack and they did make inroads into French territory but the French largely kept their positions and discipline thanks to substantial re-enforcements and some well-placed use of artillery.

Again Germany was forced to change its tactics and for several months expended their efforts in capturing a number of French forts and attempting to capture others. For the French, much was made of their success against the odds of keeping open the only remaining road into Verdun. La Voie Sacree or the Sacred Road was the only way of bringing supplies and re-enforcements to Verdun and should it have fallen during constant German pressure, the whole situation would have become entirely untenable leading to a German victory at Verdun and opening up the whole of France to invasion.

April saw the French positions under constant waves of infantry attack though Petain was not scared to launch his own vicious counter-attacks when he was able to. German successes were becoming less significant and at a cost of ever greater casualties. In June, the Germans took the heights overlooking both sides of the river and this led to an unprecedented phase of fighting as they focused on Fort Vaux.

The fort had been modernised relatively recently with reinforced concrete and its defence was led by Major Sylvain-Eugene Raynal. He led a legendary defence that continued long after the outer levels had been battered and blown away by German 16-inch howitzers. Totally besieged and having had the fort defences broken, the brave defenders created barricades in the tunnels and corridors within and under the fort. The fight continued despite poisoned drinking water and the remaining French only surrendered when their ammunition, medical supplies and food had run out.

The actions at Fort Vaux were a microcosm of the French efforts across the whole of the Verdun theatre of operations and the valour of Major Raynal was recognised by his opponents when he was awarded an officer's sword by a Crown Prince of the German Royal Family.

The fierce fighting at Verdun continued with each side gaining a temporary advantage, for example, the town of Fleury changed hands 16 times between mid-June and mid-August. June 23rd saw the Germans reach the limit of their advances at Verdun and with only Fort Souville remaining in French hands even Petain was making plans for evacuations when on 1st July Verdun was saved and the course of the war on the Western Front changed forever. The British launched the Battle of the Somme and from then on Germany was forced to focus its energies there.

However, the Battle of Verdun continued through the tail end of the summer and new counter-attack strategies allowed the French to slowly regain their lost ground and re-capture their forts including Fort Vaux.

From the start of the battle, the German military opinion was that France was at breaking point and that one huge and overwhelming battle would see it destroy their capacity to resist. Germany strategic planners wanted to emulate their successful policy they had fought against Russia in the previous year and inflict tremendous casualties on France so that they could as Falkenhayn put "France will bleed to death". They hoped to make the French army to collapse and if necessary force Britain into an ill-thought-out and rash counter-offensive which would easily be defeated and in the process ending the Entente Cordiale between the two allies.

Whilst the French leadership had long been pressuring for a

major British attack to take the pressure of the French at Verdun, Britain prevaricated until its forces were more ready (though still earlier than would have occurred without the French pressure) and this both encouraged Germany and lowered the French morale. When in fact hostilities started in the Somme, Germany at first saw it as the last throw of the dice of the Allies and particularly of Britain who was seen as the primary Allied power.

Germany also underestimated the determination of the French who were unwilling to give up having lost so many men in the battle. It was later claimed by a German Chief of The General Staff, Eric Von Falkenhayn, that his intention wasn't an overwhelming victory but instead to bleed the French Army dry. No official papers have ever been found that substantiate this claim but in many ways bleeding the French Army is sadly what happened. Verdun is the longest battle in human history and despite the massive casualties, at its ending the front lines of France and Germany were only a few hundred yards away from where they had started.

10 THE BATTLE OF THE SOMME

The Battle of The Somme sends chills down the spines of everyone who know anything about military history. With over 1 million casualties, it is simply one of the very bloodiest battles in the history of mankind and one that epitomises the bloody and futile slaughter that is a signature of The Great War.

The battle had long since been planned as a joint British and French effort against the Germans on the Western Front but when Germany engaged France at Verdun, many of the French units were diverted there, leaving The Somme to be a predominantly British affair.

The Somme is also notable for the first use of tanks and also the use of air-power. Though the Allies succeeded in pushing the Germans 6 miles back it came at the most terrible cost and General Sir Douglas Haig was criticised for his tactics, the loss of life and failure to achieve objectives almost immediately and these criticism continue to the present day.

The Germans were well dug in with numerous lines of defence and the widespread introduction of telephones allowed each sector commander to communicate with the Generals further back. The British decided on the tactic of launching a massive five-day long artillery barrage onto the German front lines. Incredibly they fired 1.6 million shells in those few days and it was hoped that this terrible bombardment would lead to an easy British victory.

However after the initial shells landed, the Germans

retreated underground, safe in the knowledge that the British couldn't attack on foot until the shelling stopped. When at last, the British troops went over the top and entered no-mans land, the British commanders were so confident that they ordered their troops to walk slowly towards the German lines. In reality most of the German troop strength was unaffected and the bombardment had only had the effect of making no-mans land entirely battered making it in many places impassable. To make matters worse, much of the barbed wire remained intact and the advancing Tommies had to either cut them as they advanced under fire or worse get stuck there and look for a gap in the defences.

There were 13 British Divisions lined up ready for action at The Somme with five more from France facing off against over ten divisions of Germans. At 7.20am the first of the massive British mines went off under no-mans land with others going off at 7.28am just two minutes before the planned offensive. They were intended to shock the German troops and provide cover for the British troops though one mine went off too late and blew up Allied soldiers as they were passing overhead. These were the biggest man-made explosions of all time and could be heard in London, 300 miles away, where they made windows rattle as the soil was thrown 4,000 feet up into the air. All day the intense noise from the 250,000 British artillery shells fired on that first day could be heard back in England.

The Battle of The Somme was to last 141 days but it all started in earnest at 7.30am on 1st July when throughout the long front line whistles were blown to signal the start of the attack. With the shelling over, the Germans left their bunkers and set up their positions.

Due to the inexperience of the British recruits, the British General Sir Henry Rawlinson rather contemptuously believed they were not up to attacking the German positions at speed and so they had been ordered to walk calmly across no-mans land due to the expectation that there would be no German resistance. As the British walked towards the German lines, the machine guns started firing and the mass slaughter began as Musketier Karl Blenk of the German 169th regiment recalled.

"We were very surprised to see them walking, we had never seen that before," he told the British historian, Martin Middlebrook, more than a half-century later.

"I could see them everywhere. There were hundreds. The officers were in front. I noticed one of them walking calmly, carrying a walking stick," he went on.

"When we started firing, we just had to reload and reload. They went down in their hundreds. We didn't have to aim, we just fired into them. If only they had run, they would have overwhelmed us."

Although a few British units managed to reach German trenches, they could not exploit their gains. Ironically the only British units that fared well that day were those whose junior officers had broken their orders. The men from Ulster were ordered by their commanding officer to run across no-mans land and they had also been told to ditch their 60lb packs before doing so. This allowed them to spring across in a matter of seconds. Similarly, another group of men had already entered no-mans land whilst the artillery barrage was still in action and so when the firing ceased they were able to reach the German front lines relatively unscathed.

By the end of the day, the British had suffered 60,000 casualties, of whom 20,000 were dead: their largest single loss. Sixty per cent of all officers involved on that first day were killed. Not all of this was due to terrible tactics; the British simply didn't realise that the height advantage which the Germans positions had in the relatively higher ground meant that the Germans were in some cases able to see what was going on in British positions and so prepare their defences accordingly.

The Germans had largely discounted any French attack and the early French artillery strikes damaged and destroyed many German guns and equipment leaving the way open for the French troops to make relatively rapid progress. Later in the morning, the French let off a large mine and simultaneously launched a gas attack which caught many of the German soldiers sheltering underground. The French advance was much more successful than the British. They had more guns and faced weaker German defences yet without similar advances by the British, they were unable to exploit their gains and were compelled to fall back to earlier positions.

It was a baptism of fire for Britain's new volunteer armies. Many 'Pals' Battalions, comprising men from the same town, had enlisted together to serve together. They suffered catastrophic losses particularly in the Serre sector with whole units dying together.

The planned and hoped for 'decisive breakthrough' was now a decisive failure and General Haig decided that attacks would concentrate on the southern sector with the British taking the German positions there on the 14th July. For two months there was a bloody stalemate with the Allies gaining little ground until on 15th September Haig ordered a renewed the offensive which for the first time made use of tanks. These tanks, however, were few in number, lightly armed and, unfortunately, liable to mechanical failure meaning that they made less impact than what they should have.

October saw the weather take a turn for the worse and continued torrential rain turned the battlegrounds into a muddy quagmire and in by the middle of November the battle petered out with the Allies having advanced only five or six miles. Only in the sense of stopping a French collapse at Verdun can the British have claimed any measure of success which in human terms was an unmitigated disaster.

Some historians believe that this war of attrition wore down the German Army so that it never again recovered to be the force it was before The Somme and that it set up the British Army for not just the rest of The Great War but for WW2 and the more recent operations. With the technology of the time as opposed to that which came slightly later on, there is also an argument that there were few alternatives for the Allied generals who had to find a way past the stalemate on the Western Front.

The Somme wasn't just one megalithic battle but rather series of smaller battles and campaigns that play as a role-call in WW1 history: Albert, Fromelles, and Delville Wood or Devils Wood as the British called it as the trees were entirely destroyed and because the ground became to resemble hell on earth. It was also notable for the introduction of South African and Rhodesian soldiers. Other cursed names include but are not limited to Serre, Morval, Ancre Heights and Thiepval where on 1st July every year, commemorations are held to the fallen of the Somme.

The Somme is the blackest name in British military history and even in WW1 can only be compared to the Battle of Verdun for the casualty rate and intensity of artillery shelling. Let us hope its awful casualty list will never be surpassed.

11 THE WAR AT SEA

For centuries, the Royal Navy had ruled the waves and the Battle of Trafalgar in 1805 solidified that dominance for the next century. The publication of the book 'The Influence of Sea Power Upon History' which theorised that Britain and its Empire controlled the world due to its navy was influential not just on Germany but the United States and Japan too with all three embarking on a battleship building programme. When the British supported Japanese Navy defeated Russia in a Naval battle, no further proof was needed for Germany, who decided a strong navy was the only way not only to grow their own empire and not be forced to depend on British goodwill to keep their trade routes open.

The British believed there were five strategic seaways that were vital to not only keeping control of the seas but also to safeguard their own trade and supply requirements. These were Dover, Gibraltar, Alexandria, Singapore and the Cape of Good Hope at South Africa.

By 1909, it was clear that a naval arms race was taking place between Germany and Britain as it was leaked to the press how senior German officials had in the past visited Portsmouth harbour and were on the way to almost matching the Royal Navy in its numbers of Capital ships. There was a public outcry in Britain with demands to build more ships, as Winston Churchill put it "The Admiralty had demanded six ships; the economists offered four; and we finally compromised on eight".

Though there were naval actions around the world in WW1, the war at sea was based around one key principle. The Royal Navy tried to keep the German surface fleet blockaded in its own waters. Even with their powerful navy, the Germans wanted to avoid any large set piece battle and instead hoped to pick off small squadrons of British vessels in an attempt to lower their numbers and allow a German blockade of the British Isles to be enacted.

As an island nation, the United Kingdom was singularly vulnerable to a naval blockade and as such it made military sense for the Germans to try and do this. The fact that they were unsuccessful however meant that the Royal Navy was able to severely limit the amount of supplies and raw materials to Germany which was vital to the war ending when it did.

The scene of the most pivotal battles was the North Sea and it was from Scapa Flow in the Orkneys that The British Grand Fleet was stationed. Aircraft carriers were only in their earliest forms at this time and so tactics and battles were dominated by Battleships, Dreadnoughts, Battle-cruisers and torpedo boats. Led by Admiral Sir John Jellicoe, the Royal Navy didn't succeed in destroying the Imperial German Navy in any decisive action such as at Trafalgar but nevertheless fought three major battles in the North Sea.

Admiral Alred Von Tirpitz had been planning his naval tactics since the end of the 19th century and assumed the Royal Navy would either attack Germany outright or put in place a very close blockade which could then be picked off by U-Boats. It was also assumed that Britain would have its navy spread around the world when in reality a massive ship-building programme meant the Royal Navy had ample ships in home-waters. When Britain decided to blockade Germany but from a distance, Turpitz's plans had in effect been blown out of the water from the start.

Just a few weeks after the United Kingdom entered the war, 54 ships of the Royal Navy including 5 Battlecruisers and 33 Destroyers confronted 37 German naval vessels in the first of two battles near Heligoland, a former British island base just off the German coast on August 28th 1914. The result was a complete British victory with 6 German vessels sank, six others badly damaged and the loss of 712 German lives with the British suffering just one damaged vessel and 35 deaths.

Still in the early days of the war, the Germans took the offensive not just to the Royal Navy but to Great Britain itself. Following a minor and ineffectual raid on Great Yarmouth in October, on December 16th 1914, the Imperial German Navy managed to reach the north-east coast of England and launched a naval barrage onto the towns of Hartlepool, West Hartlepool, Scarborough and Whitby. The attack caught Britain by surprise and resulted in 137 fatalities and 592 injuries with children as young as six months old being killed. The attack caused a national outrage and a general opinion that Germany had committed a war crime by deliberately targeting civilians.

In 1915, another significant battle occurred at Dogger Bank, a shallow area of the North Sea where in prehistoric times people once lived. Squadrons of the British and German navies fought on 24th January 1915. Victory belonged again to the Royal Navy though the battle suffered from tactical and operational errors on both sides with just 1 German Battlecruiser being sank for the loss of 954 lives.

The sea battle that is always remembered when World War One comes to mind is the Battle of Jutland. It was the biggest naval battle of the war though one with a less than decisive victory. Though primarily fought between the

British Grand Fleet and the German High Seas Fleet, personnel and ships from Canada and Australia were also involved with their British Allies.

The battle was fought on 31stMay-1st June 1916 and was conceived as a way for Germany to break the blockade that was strangling their trade and supplies of raw materials. The British caught the Germans off-guard but the vanguard of its fleet was lured towards the German fleet by a small scouting squadron and several vessels were sunk. The British ships returned towards their main fleet when they saw it was a trick which was the cue for the main German Fleet to follow in pursuit. The ongoing battle was terrible with heavy casualties on both sides. The smoke and oil from the ships made it difficult for anyone to get a clear view of what was going on and it pushed both men and ship to the peak of their endurance.

During the night, the British manoeuvred and hoped to get between the Germans and their home bases but somehow the German vessels manage to slip through a lightly populated part of the fleet and escape home.

There were 151 British ships and 99 German ships and by nightfall the British had lost 14 ships and 6,094 deaths whilst the Germans 11 vessels and 2,551 deaths.

Criticism was made of Vice-Admiral David Beatty who led the initial foray and had the German vessels within range of his superior ships for 10 minutes whilst the Germans could not reach him, despite that, he didn't fire and lost an early opportunity to shape the battle. There was much dissatisfaction in the U.K. that the Royal Navy did not achieve a decisive victory by stopping the Germans retreating during the night. Though Germany and Britain claimed a victory, in reality despite suffering less losses than the British, the Germans failed to achieve their goal of destroying a notable section of the Royal Navy and to break the blockade. For much of the rest of the war the German fleet hid in home waters behind its mine-fields. It was happy to challenge Russia in the east but not to confront Britain again head to head and this allowed the British to slowly strangle Germany in everything from munitions factories to food for the civil population.

There were few naval encounters in the English Channel whilst in the Atlantic the Germans used their U-boat fleet to sink hundreds of merchant vessels and even passenger liners which broke the Hague Conventions. Their attacks on the vessels of even neutral nations such as the United States hardened opinion against Germany and the Axis powers in general.

There were some minor engagements in the Mediterranean Sea but the Ottoman Empire was reluctant to confront the British and French navies, besides which, it had enough to contend with in The Black Sea where there was a major Russian naval base. The Ottoman Fleet was going through a period of modernisation as much of its fleet was aged. Unfortunately for it, when war was declared, its two new state of the art vessels being built in the U.K. were confiscated and put into action for the Royal Navy. In October 1914, the Ottoman Fleet bombarded the Russian Black Sea Coast and for much of the war the two empires conducted a very tactical and sporadic series of naval engagements. The Ottomans advantage of individually more powerful ships was gradually reduced by the increasing number of Russian vessels but in 1916 the Russians managed to lay mines across the entrance to the

Black Sea in effect stopping any naval action there until the Russians left the war.

The Royal Navy operated a number of submarines in the Black Sea and Mediterranean as it did in the Baltic Sea in support of Russia but the Baltic was primarily the battleground between Germany and Russia. In August 1914, the Axis cruiser SMS Magdeburg ran aground in the Gulf of Finland in dense fog. Despite efforts by the Germans, the ship couldn't be saved and instead was scuttled. Shortly afterwards Russian Navy divers searched the wreck and recovered a German Code Book which when passed to the Royal Navy was most important in containing the German threat in the North Sea. Germany utilised its Navy effectively by using it in support of its ground attacks on the Baltic States and in the Battle of Moon Sound sank the Russian Battleship Slava.

Several German ships were already overseas upon the start of the war and they spent much of the war raiding coastal cities such as Madras in India and attacking Allied shipping. More importantly was the German East-Asia Squadron led by Vice-Admiral Maximilian Von Spree, who raided locations in the Pacific before defeating a small British force off the coast of Chile in the Battle of Coronel. A Royal Navy task force was immediately sent to meet them which they did at the Battle of The Falklands on 8th December 1914 just as the German force was set to attack Port Stanley. The result was a stunning victory for the Royal Navy with 6 of the 8 German vessels destroyed and the remainder forced to flee to neutral Chile where they were later destroyed.

As Allied Naval forces led the capture of many of the more isolated German colonies, the remaining German forces were left without supply depots. One of the most unusual naval engagements took place in Lake Tanganyika in East Africa where Germany was fighting British and Belgian forces. The lake was home to two German warships that sunk the only Belgian vessel and British postal ship in 1914.The Germans made great use of the large lake by raiding Allied forces on all sides of it. When in 1915, news emerged that they were launching and new warship from their fortified port of Kigoma named the Graf Von Gotzen, the Admiralty decided something had to be done as it was the duty of the Royal Navy to fight anyway there was enough water for an enemy vessel to be floated!

The man chosen to lead this mission was Geoffrey Spicer-Simpson, who had overseen a number of disasters despite rising through the ranks. He is memorably described by Giles Foden as "a man court-martialled for wrecking his own ships, an inveterate liar and a wearer of skirts"!

Two 40 foot long boats named Mimi and Toutou (Spicer-Simpson'a original plan to name them cat and dog was rejected by the Admiralty and so he picked these names which mean 'Miaow' and 'Bow-wow" in French) were sent to Cape Town where along with a small force were transported northwards by railway. They were then towed 146 miles by teams of Oxen and steam engines until they found navigable waterways.

On December 26th 1915, the British captured the German ship Kingani and after burying its dead crew, repaired it and enlisted it to their force as HMS Fifi which Spicer-Simpson declared was French for 'tweet-tweet'. Shortly afterwards HMS Fifi sank the German vessel Hedwig.

It wasn't until July 26th 1916 when after being attacked from the air that the Gotzen was taken out of action, its crew filling her with concrete and scuttling her. Amazingly, the British re-floated her after the war and the Gotzen still sails upon Lake Tanganyika under her assumed name of Liemba.

Once hostilities had ceased at the end of The Great War, the German High Seas Fleet was interned in the Royal Navy Base at Scapa Flow in the Orkney Islands off the northeast coast of Scotland. There were negotiations over what to do with the fleet and after 9 months of waiting and fearing his vessels would all be divided amongst the Allies (something the Americans and French wanted whilst Britain wanted them all destroyed) and unaware that an extension of the talks had been granted, Rear-Admiral von Reuter began plans to scuttle his fleet.

At 11.20am on June 21st 1919, the order was given by von Reuter to scuttle his fleet and 52 of the vessels sank whilst the Royal Navy managed to salvage the remainder though in the process 9 German sailors were killed as they temporarily came under fire and so became the final casualties of WW1.

The Americans and particularly the French were unhappy at the loss of the ships, The British pleased as it secured their huge numeric advantage over everyone else and the German admirals pleased that their honour had been preserved with the majority of their fleet not falling into enemy hands.

Today the wrecks of the German vessels are a big attraction for deep sea divers though care must be taken not to disturb the Royal Navy vessels which were sank nearby in WW2 and are classified as a war-grave.

12 THE HOME FRONT

Whilst the war was primarily one fought overseas and putting aside the casualties from naval bombardments and air-raids, the war at home also brought unheralded changes. World War One was the first of what is now known as 'Total War' and a total war requires total commitment from an entire nation. Obviously, one of the biggest effects that the war has on civilian life is that of the changing role of women which is dealt with in the following chapter.

Politics

As early as the 8th August 1914, the government introduced The Defence of the Realm Act, which brought in wide-ranging powers allowing the state to gain acquisition of land and materials for the war-effort. A number of restrictions were brought in limiting civilian movements and preventing individuals from discussing many military activities. Pub closing times were introduced, alcohol watered down and British Summer Time introduced.

The government was led Prime Minister Herbert Asquith of the Liberal Party and it was seen as being largely ineffectual in taking the tough decisions needed in war time. Despite dreadful casualties, the war on the Western Front had stagnated by 1916, Gallipoli and Mesopotamia had been disastrous campaigns and there was a shortage of high calibre ammunition. The country was beginning to run out of funds to obtain American supplies and it was time for a change in government.

Political manoeuvrings saw Liberal PM David Lloyd George head-up a coalition government which contained more Conservative ministers than his own Liberal members. He brought incredible vigour to the establishment was sufficiently focused and energised to properly manage the war for the first time and it isn't a co-incidence that following his arrival, the long drawn out stale-mates and bloody set-piece battles began to give way to more tactical and mobile battles which culminated with the end of the war.

In the spring of 1918 with a reversal of German fortunes, a fall-out from the Irish conscription crisis and an aggrieved former PM Asquith, the government came under renewed criticism. The Liberal party began to implode with the newly emerging Labour Party gaining support and Lloyd George having to increasingly adopt the policies of his mainly Conservative government.

Despite this, Lloyd George led his coalition into the 1918 General Election and was successful against his fellow Liberal opponents. Herbert Asquith and many other Liberals lost their seats and the Liberal Party lost its support to the Labour Party and was to remain largely irrelevant until it again formed a coalition government in 2010.

Throughout WW1, the Labour Party was a relatively minor political force though it had been helped by the Liberal decision to introduce a wage for Members of Parliament and in 1910 won 42 MPs. The Labour Party was still a growing force though it had already made an impact throughout the early years of the century by supporting a series of Liberal welfare reforms which were a precursor to the modern welfare state.

Mostly the Labour Party was then a force in local councils and they strongly worked towards helping the unemployed and improving housing for the poor and fair wages for the working class. The party itself was split over WW1 and became increasingly anti-war as the conflict progressed. The Labour leader and eventual first Labour Prime Minister Ramsay Macdonald was an avowed anti-war campaigner, resigned his position as head of the parliamentary party.

The mainstream Labour Party, however, was generally supportive of the Coalition government and under the Lloyd George administration became involved at a ministerial level as the Prime Minster was anxious to keep Trade Union support for the war effort. They were also influential in attacking profiteering, price controls on food and fixing rents at pre-war levels. Their success combined with a Liberal Party at war with itself allowed it to increase support outside Trade Unions to the workers themselves and women. In 1922 they won 142 seats at the General Election and became the Official Opposition Party before forming their first government under Ramsay Macdonald in 1924.

The Economy

Unlike Germany whose economy contracted by 27% during the war, Great Britain's increased by 19% thanks to the import of large amounts of American raw materials and deep inroads into the national reserves as well as international loans.

Inflation sent prices soaring across the world and though the economic powerhouse of London helped with inflation, families found many everyday items and food, in particular, to be hard to come by.

People were encouraged to grow vegetables in their gardens and the government tried their best not to introduce restrictions and even when they did in 1916, they were limited in there severity. Increased German U-Boat activity in 1917 meant the King and Queen led a voluntary rationing programme in February but as the situation worsened, mandatory rationing for food and fuel was introduced by the end of the year. Ration cards were issued and people were required to register with their local butchers and grocers.

By 1918 with their being only a few weeks of food reserves in the country such basic items as sugar, butter, meat, cheese and margarine were put on the ration list. It made life tough for everyone but it worked, the country continued to function through the final months of the war and no-one actually starved in Britain during the Great War although a significant section of the population was suffering from severe malnutrition by the time the war was over.

Ireland

The decades leading up to the WW1 saw increasing moves towards some sort of Irish self-rule possibly within the United Kingdom. Whilst some Irish wanted full independence, the average Irish man or women in 1900 did not particularly want independence but like the working classes of mainland Britain, simply political and social reforms. The Great War however arrived at a bad time for the British government which understandably found its attention distracted by the war and was unable to put into place policies which might have kept Ireland united and within the U.K.

At the start of the war 180,000 Irish men volunteered to fight for their King and country and even the Catholic Church supported them in their efforts to stop the rape of Catholic Belgium by Germany. Despite this, Irish Nationalists were adept at causing mischief and furthering discontent and as in India, there were even plots by Germany to stir up civil unrest.

On the morning of April 24th 1916, what became known as the Easter Rising took place when approximately 1,200 nationalist volunteers took over Dublin city centre. Republican flags were raised and Ireland was declared a republic. The nationalists overtook many key points in Dublin including the courts, hospitals and public squares but despite killing a sentry and overpowering the guards on duty, failed to take Dublin Castle, which was the seat of military power in Ireland.

Unionists managed to hold Trinity College and when some Irish citizens attempted to remove Republican barricades some were physically beaten off and others shot dead. Initial British attempts to regain control were largely small-scale and uncoordinated as they hadn't expected the uprising and so had no plans to put into action to reverse it.

As the nationalists hadn't taken control of the ports or train stations, it enabled a fast re-enforcement of British troops from England. After a series of vicious small-scale assaults, the heavily outnumbered nationalists were forced to surrender.

Despite Ireland being a full component of Great Britain in WW1, politicians had tried to avoid conscription in the territory which would be seen as politically and socially problematic. However by 1918, the British Army was in the midst of a severe numbers crisis and reluctantly a decision was taken to introduce conscription in Ireland. Prime Minister Lloyd George tied in the conscription ruling into an Irish Home Rule policy in an attempt to placate the Irish.

However, this only had the effect of upsetting both sides of the debate with Irish who didn't want to fight and Irish who were happy with British rule and didn't want to change the system of governance.

The situation caused an outrage amongst much of the Irish population despite the fact that countless Irish men had volunteered to fight for their country which at that time was the United Kingdom of Great Britain and Ireland. A General Strike was held on 23rd April 1918 which brought war-time production in Ireland to a halt and there were several anti-conscription rallies during the following months.

With American entry into the war, Irish Conscription was abandoned; the number of men involved in any case almost inconsequential with the looming tide of soldiers from the United States. The discontent it caused was one of the reasons that set the scene for eventual independence for the southern Irish counties.

Conscientious Objection

As the war continued and the initial flood of volunteers to the Armed Forced ran dry, the government decided to introduce conscription to make up the numbers for all of the men who had died.

There was a public right to avoid conscription to active military service if individuals could prove themselves to be Conscientious Objectors. Even if a strong patriotic and civic had allowed such a feeling, it was not enough to simply refuse to fight because they didn't want to. Instead such minded individuals had to convince a Military Tribunal of the strength of their convictions. Those with a history of pacifism, especially through religious beliefs such as

Quakers were much more likely to escape with doing vital work on farms or other industries essential to the war effort. Those with less convincing arguments were coerced to serve in non-combat roles such as stretcher bearers. It wasn't easy to convince the tribunal and the vast majority were ordered to fight and 6,000 who refused to obey orders were sent to prison. Others were given death sentences which were commuted to life imprisonment. Altogether just 17,000 British men invoked the Conscientious Objection clause and successful objectors were often shunned at home and given white feathers, a sign of cowardice.

Part of the reason there were so few who objected to combat roles is due to the wealth of propaganda both direct from the government or from strongly patriotic newspapers and magazines. Even popular music became patriotic to raise the morale of the public and serving soldiers alike. Songs like "It's a long way to Tipperary" and "Pack up your troubles in your kit bag" became popular in music halls across the country and are one of the few aspects of popular culture of WW1 that we are still familiar with today.

Social Change and the Aristocracy

The most important aristocratic family in the whole world was, of course, the Royal Family and when war broke out, they immediately suffered an image problem. It was closely linked by blood to the Kaiser in Germany and its official family name was the House of Saxe-Coburg and Gotha which reflected the current Royals ancestral links with Germany. There was widespread public uproar and by July 1917, King George V mandated that henceforth all the royals descended from Queen Victoria would take the surname 'Windsor'. Many royals were ordered to drop their German heraldic titles altogether or have them anglicised so that the kings cousin Prince Louis of Battenberg, overnight became Louis Mountbatten, 1st Marquess of Milford Haven, while his brother-in-law, the Duke of Teck, became Adolphus Cambridge, 1st Marquess of Cambridge. Those royal family members who maintained links with or even fought for Germany were simply cut off by an act of parliament.

It wasn't just the Royal Family that was affected, WW1 permanently changed the life of the landed aristocracy. Many families lost most of their male servants and staff due to conscription and many men never returned home. Women who for centuries had been happy to work in-service found new opportunities opening to them which offered them both better pay and prospects. The way of life had changed forever and many families could no longer run their own estates. New taxes were introduced that targeted the wealthy land-owners and a growing worldwide economy and increased industrialisation meant growing numbers of estates were forced to close down, starting a trend that continued for the next 50 years.

13 WOMEN AND THE WAR

When we think of The Great War, the role of women is an often forgotten element in comparison to the famous battlefields around the world. However as the German leadership quickly stated, WW1 was a total war that required the participation of each nation to win and that included women. Not only did WW1 change the perceived role of women in Great Britain but women were crucial to the war effort itself.

Women were non-combatants in WW1 but they worked in a number of important support roles which would previously have been carried out by men if only they hadn't gone off to fight for their country.

It was their job to keep the home fires burning and by the end of 1914 over 5 million of 24 million women were working in a large variety of jobs including office jobs, farms, clothing factories and munitions factories where working women were known as Canary Girls. Many women sewed socks and other warm items of clothing for soldiers in Europe whilst others performed charity work though with no-one else to support them, women were always mindful to concentrate on paid-work so their children wouldn't starve.

Right from the beginning of the war, Britain encountered a crisis with the production of munitions for the front line. Ammunition was needed on an unprecedented scale and following the Shell Crisis of 1915; the government put in place legislation forcing munitions factories to open their doors to women. By 1917 approximately 80% of the ammunition used by the British Army was being manufactured by women in armament factories. Sometimes referred to as Munitionettes, they women were required to work with dangerous chemicals and TNT on a daily basis and with none of the safety equipment that would be used today. Repeated and prolonged exposure of their skin to Sulphuric Acid would make the women's skin glow yellow, an attribute that earned them the term 'Canary Girls'. The chemicals also would cause many chronic long-term health problems such as anaemia, liver failure and infertility and those that did babies often gave birth to yellow coloured children.

The work in the munitions factories was arduous but did give the women a feel of patriotism and of helping their men folk whilst also officially offering a salary twice as high as their previous war employments though only half the wage of a man doing the same job Unofficially however many women found ways to earn much more even than non-commission officers on the Western Front. The work there was hard, physical and repetitive and many women worked 12-hour shifts 6 or 7 days a week. Such work also presented real dangers and during the war hundreds of women died from accidental fires and explosions in the factories.

The role of women in the war effort became even more important following the introduction of conscription in 1916 when men were forcibly sent to war leaving more jobs that needed to be done. Although the trade unions ensured that these jobs were only temporary so that returning soldiers after the war would have some sort of paid employment.

The Government also invited women to join the ranks of the Women's Land Army, an organisation that offered cheap female labour to farmers who were not always happy to employ women. The 260,000 volunteers that made up the WLA were given little more than a uniform and orders to work as hard as they could. The advances in mechanical farming of the previous decades were lost as fuel restrictions made a return to manual agricultural labour unavoidable.

A typical example of a Land Girl as the WLA members came to be known is that of Agnes Greatorex from Cardiff who left the traditional role of domestic service for life at Green Farm. She recalled:

"We had to get up at five in the morning for milking, and then we'd have to take it up to Glan Ely hospital. After that - especially during the winter - we'd have to muck-out the cow sheds. Then we might get half an hour for breakfast. I'd be out there picking up stones from the field or cutting hay, and I'd be as happy as a lark."

She believed that, although her work on Green Farm was equally as arduous as that in service, being a Land Girl gave her a glimpse into the future of better prospects for women.

"When I became a Land Girl I thought that's it, I'm independent. I had a pound a week, not as much as the men but a lot still - there was no-one to boss me, no more running around at the beck and call of the cook. I think the First World War did change women. Because once they'd had a taste they wouldn't go back to service, they were free."

The role of the Land Army was particularly important when it is remembered that the U.K. only grew 35% of its annual food consumption in 1914 and the Germans tried their best to blockade the shipping routes to starve the country into submission which in the end is what the Royal Navy did to Germany. Nevertheless, it was always a fine line and at one point in 1917, there were only three weeks of food supplies in the country. Without the effort of the women on the land, it is likely that the country would either have starved, surrendered or, at least, famine would have caused widespread death and civil unrest.

It isn't widely known whether women workers understood from the beginning that their employment could only be temporary that is how it transpired. It was a similar story in other nations fighting in the war with women brought in to work in the jobs evacuated by men only to be dismissed back home to make room for the returning soldiers.

Nursing was the only section of the military that was open to women and many thousands of them joined up with several hundred being killed during the war from amongst all the Allied nations. Much of our impression of nursing in WW1 is tinged with romance with gentle, kindly young nurses in starched and white uniforms tending heroically in the Voluntary Aid Detachment or VAD.

One of the best accounts of the VAD is written by one of its most prominent members, Vera Brittain. Born into a relatively wealthy family in Newcastle-Under-Lyme, Vera was sent away to a private boarding school before gaining entrance to Oxford University but in 1915, she put her studies and career on hold to go into the VAD.

After the war, she movingly remembered her experiences in her publication 'Testament of Youth'. She was a feminist and a pacifist, partly due no doubt to the fact that she had lost all of the important men that she loved in her live including her fiancé Roland, her brother Edward and her close friends Victor and Geoffrey.

Vera threw herself into nursing in some of the most dreadful battlegrounds in an attempt to ease the pain of her multiple bereavements. She also later dedicated herself to recreating the characters and lives of those she had lost so that generations of readers would come to know them and in a way live on in the memory of the readers.

Like many others, Vera Brittain was expecting her fiancé Roland Leighton to return home on leave just after Christmas 1915. Sadly he died on December 23 of wounds received during a night-time wire inspection a day earlier. Here is an extract from a letter written by Vera to her brother Edward on January 14 1916. She had been working at the London hospital and so have been able to travel to Brighton to visit Roland's family

"I arrived at a very opportune, though very awful, moment. All Roland's things had just been sent back from the front through

Cox's; they had just opened them and they were all lying on the floor. I had no idea before of the after-results of an officer's death, or what the returned kit, of which so much has been written in the papers, really meant. It was terrible. Mrs Leighton and Clare were both crying as bitterly as on the day we heard of his death, and Mr Leighton with his usual instinct was taking all the things everybody else wanted and putting them where nobody could ever find them. (His doings always seem to me to supply the slight element of humour which makes tragedy so much more tragic.)

These were his clothes - the clothes in which he came home from the front last time. Everything was damp and worn and simply caked with mud. And I was glad that neither you, nor Victor, nor anyone else who may some day go to the front was there to see. If you had been you would have been overwhelmed by the horror of war without its glory. For though he had only worn the things when living, the smell of those clothes was the smell of graveyards and the dead. The mud of France which covered them was not ordinary mud; it had not the usual clean pure smell of earth, but it was as though it were saturated with dead bodies - dead that had been dead a long, long time. All the sepulchres and catacombs of Rome could not make me realise mortality and decay and corruption as vividly as did the smell of those clothes. I know now what he meant when he used to write of "this refuse-heap of a country" or "a trench that is nothing but a charnel-house.

We discovered that the bullet was an expanding one. The hole where it went in in front - well below where the belt would have been, just below the bottom right-hand pocket of the tunic - was almost microscopic, but at the back, almost exactly where his back bone would have been, there was quite a large rent. The under things he was wearing at the time have evidently had to be destroyed, but they sent back a khaki waistcoat or vest ... which was dark and stiff with blood, and a pair of khaki breeches also in the same state, which had been slit open at the top by someone in a great hurry - probably the doctor in haste to get at the wound, or perhaps even by one of the men. Even the tabs of his braces were blood-stained. He must have fallen on his back, as in every case the back of his clothes was much more stained and muddy than the front.

The charnel-house smell seemed to grow stronger and stronger till it pervaded the room and obliterated everything else. Finally, Mrs Leighton said, "Robert, take those clothes away into the kitchen, and don't let me see them again; I must either burn or bury them. They smell of death; they are not Roland, they seem to detract from his memory and spoil his glamour. I won't have any more to do with them."

And indeed, one could never imagine those things the same as those in which he had lived and walked. One couldn't believe anyone alive had been in them at all. No, they were not him. After the clothes had gone we opened the window wide and felt better, but it was a long time before the smell and even the taste of them went away."

After the war, Vera went on to write a number of acclaimed works on her experiences in the war. She also became an active speaker at the League of Nations and joined several pacifist organisations. She lived until the 1970's and when she died she had her ashes scattered on the grave of her brother in Italy who she had loved so much and missed for so many years.

Elsewhere, the main trained corps of military nurses in the British Army was the Queen Alexandra's Imperial Military Nursing Service (QAIMNS). It was founded in during the Boer War in South Africa in 1902 and at the time of the start of WW1 was less than 300 strong. At the end of the war four years later it numbered over 10,000 nurses. There were also several other organisations formed earlier in the century focused on the nursing of injured members of the military such as the First Aid Nursing Yeomanry launched in 1907.

With the exception of the QAIMNS, the British Army was resolutely opposed to nursing units comprised entirely of women and so many of the early female volunteers from Britain instead served with the French and Belgian forces. Many of these early volunteers were either from aristocratic families or their servants. Such women who ran large families and large estates were well versed in management and saw no great problems in managing a military hospital instead. Their powerful positions at home gave them a natural confidence in their abilities at war.

Perhaps the most famous of these aristocratic women was the Duchess of Sutherland who was nicknamed Meddlesome Millie. Soon after war was declared she and other Ladies like her took doctors and nurses to France and Belgium, organising their own transport and equipment to set up hospitals and casualty clearing stations.

Whatever bureaucratic obstacles were put in their way, the huge and bloody tide of casualties by the spring of 1915 simply swept them away. Even the British Army's top brass yielded to the combined pressures of desperation and strong, confident commitment.

When the government encouraged greater female participation in all sections of employment, thousands of young women from middle-class homes with little experience of domestic work, not much relevant education and total ignorance of male bodies, volunteered and found themselves pitched into military hospitals. In many instances they not made to feel welcome and professional nurses who had long battled for some kind of recognition and better training feared this large invasion of unqualified volunteers would undermine their efforts.

VADs were usually very poorly paid and were often used primarily as domestic labour, cleaning floors, changing bed linen, swilling out bedpans, but were rarely allowed until later in the war to change dressings or administer drugs. Relations between professional nurses and the volunteer assistants were constrained by rigid and unbending discipline. Contracts for VADs could be withdrawn even for slight breaches of the rules.

A sometimes forgotten part of the experience of women in WW1 is that it fell primarily to them to adjust to life after the war and hold the country together. Millions across Europe in particular didn't return home and hundred of thousands of men who did get back home were injured in some way. Women bore a large part of the burden of caring for these men whilst dealing with continuing without their fathers, husbands, lovers, brothers, and sons. All the time life had to go on, the country had to be rebuilt and children and families had to get back into normal life no matter how difficult it was.

For all of this the women did the see advancement of their status and position in society. The Suffragette movement had reached an agreement with the government at the start of WW1 and a cessation of protests was ordered though the movement remained strong with a continual though peaceful campaign for change. Their patience and hard work was rewarded by the 1918 Representation of the People Act, which granted the vote to women over 30 who owned property, giving women a voice in government for the first time.

Soon after this the Sex Disqualification (Removal) Act of 1919, made it illegal to exclude women from jobs because of their gender, opening the doors to women of all classes to enter previously male-dominated professions.

Mrs Millicent Fawcett, president of the National Union of Women's Suffrage Societies from 1897-1918 described that "The War revolutionised the industrial position of women – it found them serfs and left them free".

It's a common held view that women achieved universal suffrage in 1928 solely because of their role in WW1 which made men realise that women were capable of working in the wider world. However whilst WW1 helped narrow their pay-gap to just two-thirds of the male wage, it can be argued that women were always likely to get the vote following the decision to give the vote to the working class soldiers.

14 NEW WEAPONS OF WAR

It is often said that necessity is the mother of invention and rarely are inventions more necessary than in times of war. One of the reasons that the death-toll of WW1 is so great, particularly in Europe is that for much of the war the armies fought with modern 20th Century weaponry but they had not yet developed modern tactics to deal with it.

Many of the generals were simply naive or even uncaring as to the suffering and death toll of the lower ranks. Previously Generals had led wars on the battlefields, but now the scope of battles was so large that the only way they could get a proper overview and manage events effectively was from some distance by way of the newly invented telephones, telegraphs and carrier pigeons. Though there are many cases of unthinkably bad leadership in WW1, even a military genius would be hard pressed to beat the stalemate on the western front with no prior experience of this new style war and with the weapons and technology available. However gradually scientific advancements and new thinking came up with ways to break the deadlock.

Some of the terrible weapons of WW1 were not new at all. Machine Guns, though increasingly deadly and able to 600 rounds per minute had their forebears in the 19th Century Gatling Guns.

Although invented millennia earlier, WW1 saw the perfected use of flame throwers by the German Army. They were first used at the Battle of Verdun and were an effective way of neutralising the defenders of any particular trench. Unlike hand grenades, flame-throwers had the bonus of not damaging the structural integrity of the defences which was useful because once captured, they could quickly be re-used by their new owners.

Another breakthrough in war technology was that of tracer bullets invented by the British in 1915. Tracer bullets let off small amounts of flammable material that left a phosphorescent trail allowing improved accuracy of night fighting as the shooters could see where their bullets were going. Additionally, the flammable contents were perfect for shooting down zeppelins and observer balloons.

It wasn't just on the land and obviously in the air where there were improvements but on the sea too. The first air-craft carriers were created even though their take-off and landing areas were often just quick and primate modifications of existing vessels. Hydrophones allowed the detection of German U-boats underwater whilst the Royal Navy invented Depth Charges to attack U-boats. They worked by dropping an explosive charge with a pressure switch that would go off at a pre-planned depth. Obviously, it was partly down to luck as to how effective it was, particularly without sonar but it was the only real weapon going against submarines and on 22nd March 1916, U-68 was the first vessel to be destroyed in this way.

Perhaps the two greatest or indeed most terrible inventions were that of tanks and poison gas. Tanks continue with us to this day as valid weapons of war whilst poison gasses have long since been banned and only used by the worst of despots such as Saddam Hussein and President Assad of Syria.

The use of poison gas or chemical weapons as it would now be known as is one of the timeless horrors of WW1. Not all of the gasses were poisonous, some were merely disabling, but the fact that gas was an indiscriminate weapon and one that killed people in such horrific ways means that the notoriety of the gas far exceeds the estimated 4% of WW1 casualties actually caused by it. Then as now, use of chemical weapons was a war crime thanks to the 1899 and 1907 Hague Conventions.

The first use of tear gas like substances took place in the autumn of 1914 when the French fired it at the Germans and the Germans used it against the British, but the quantities were so inadequate that they were barely noticed by either side. The Germans again used it on 31st January 1915 when they fired 18,000 shells of gas at the Russians but the temperature was so cold that the mixture simply froze.

The first reported use of deadly gas was by the Germans using concentrated Chlorine against the British just prior to an attack on 2nd January 1915 when 140 British were killed by the gas and it was reported that even German officers thought it to be a horrible weapon.

By April 1915, the Germans had 168 tonnes of Chlorine just north of Ypres. One of the problems with the gas was that it was carried by the wind and so on occasion would drift back towards those who released it. On 22nd April, the Germans targeted a position near Ypres held by French Colonial troops who fled when they saw the approaching gas leaving a 7km gap in the front line. It was not exploited however as the Germans were fearful of running into the gas and so no progress could be made before the Allies regrouped.

Poison gas was also used several times against the British during the second battle of Ypres 21st April – 25th May causing 90 deaths in the trenches and many more at the casualty stations, some of which suffered slow, painful deaths. Whilst in October of the same year more than 1,000 Russians died in Poland after a similar German attack near Warsaw.

It soon became noticeable that those who ran about in the gas suffered worse than those who stood still and exertion and increased breathing obviously increased the gas absorption into the lungs and body. Standing still on top of the trench could result in almost not suffering any ill-effects but as the gas was heavier than air it could drop into the trenches and those who tried to hide from it or wounded on the floor of the trench would suffer the worse effects.

Chlorine, in particular, could not only be protected against by gas masks but in an emergency by a water soaked cloth. There are even reports of urine soaked cloths being excellent protectors as chlorine is water soluble.

The British were outraged by the use of poison gas against them, but the Germans denied that they were breaking the Hague convention that they claimed didn't outlaw gas. They therefore set up their own research programme to use against the Germans though their first use on 25th September 1915 in the Battle of Loos was a disaster. Their front line troops couldn't open all the gas canisters and what gas did get released got stuck in No-Mans Land and parts even came back onto the British when the wind changed. Finally German retaliatory shelling hit the unopened canisters releasing gas over the British lines.

Later more deadly and invisible gasses were developed and the number of deaths caused by them increased with the most infamous derivation being the German developed Mustard Gas or Hun Gas as the British called it. It would be delivered through artillery fire and exposure would cause extreme irritation to the eyes and vomiting. Skin would blister and they would suffer internal bleeding and attack the bronchial tubes. Though not fatal unless in large doses, it could often take more than a month for victims to die in the most horrendous fashion especially as they knew what was coming to them. The only major power that didn't use chemical weapons was the Unites States, primarily due to their late entry into the war. They did begin industrial production of gas for use in 1919 but never had the opportunity to use it.

Poison gas was never again used on a wide-spread scale except by Iraq during the Iran-Iraq war. However the British government was prepared to use it on the landing beaches should Nazi Germany have invaded in 1940.

Another new invention of WW1 was that of the Creeping Barrage by the British. Previously artillery has been used to blast the enemy for days on end but so long as the enemy soldiers survived the first rounds and made it to an underground bunker then they were relatively safe. When the shelling stopped, it simply telegraphed the enemy to expect an attack. Creeping Barrages were not only a clever way of breaking down the stalemate on the Western Front but were almost a weapon of terror as increasingly accurate big guns could be set to different ranges, perhaps every

10 feet over half a mile. This not only meant that no-one on open ground was safe but that the shells could constantly be aimed a few hundred yards in front of advancing British troops providing them with cover. Just before the troops reached the German front lines the artillery would be shelling the German trenches either killing troops or leaving them so confused and disorganised that they were easily overcome by the soldiers on the ground.

Perhaps the most imaginative and far-reaching development on the battlefields of World War One is that of the Landship, better known as the tank as the workers who made the first of them though they resembled steel water tanks. The first prototype was known as 'Little Willie' and was built in the August and September of 1915. Its development and eventual roll-out was strongly backed by Winston Churchill who was one of the first people in the world to recognise its potential. The first French tanks were on the battlefield by April 1917 whilst the German leadership didn't see the value in tanks at all and instead concentrated on anti-tank weaponry which by the end of the war was extremely effective.

Due to the waterlogged, muddy and cratered landscape, conventional motor vehicles were next to useless and were in any case extremely vulnerable to gunfire. The Mark 1 tank was rhomboid in shape and its long 26foot length made it able to overcome all but the roughest terrain and they had the firepower to mount withering attacks on all before them. At first tanks were prone to mechanical breakdown leaving them and their crew sitting ducks but when they worked, nothing could get in their way and ordinary gun fire was ineffective. Where tanks strove forward, swarms of soldiers could follow, hiding directly behind the tank if necessary.

Churchill's initial requirements were for his landships to be an armoured vehicle with speed of 4mph, the ability to climb a 5 foot high parapet and to cross 8 foot wide gaps with armaments including machine guns and a small artillery like cannon. A number of designs were considered including monotrack vehicles and others with extremely large wheels but in the end it was decided to use caterpillar tracks.

The first use of tanks in war was on 15th September 1916 in the Battle of Flers-Courcelette which was part of the larger Somme Battle and saw 32 British tanks set off across no-mans land although only 9 made it right across. The rough terrain meant that they often travelled only 1mph but their steel armour protected occupants from small arms and artillery fire though a direct hit by a mortar or artillery shell would immobilise them. Additionally as they used naval style guns, if the tank went down a steep crater sometimes the large gun cold get stuck in the mud! The conditions inside the first tanks were appalling as there was little ventilation or visibility and the cabin filled with petrol fumes whilst temperatures could reach 50Degree C / 122 Degree F causing crews to collapse while inside and sometime again when released back into the fresh and normal temperature air. Additionally the sound of the engine was deafening and the crew also had to put up with the sound of both their gunfire and those hitting the armour of their tank.

It is felt that tanks were not always utilised to their utmost as Field Marshal Haig was himself a cavalry man and didn't appreciate the advantages that tanks could bring but by early 1917, there were still 1,000 British tanks and there were even more French ones though the French suffered from inferior design and often were deployed less effectively than the British ones.

The British continued to develop the tanks throughout the war and by 1917 were up to the Mark 4 tank with more effective guns and armour and the Mark 5 tank meant that it no longer took four crew to steer the tank.

One of the outstanding uses of tanks in WW1 was the 1917 Battle of Cambrai when they broke through the German lines on an unprecedented scale. The Western Front was no longer static as it had been in the first years of the war and instead was beginning to take on the characteristics of later wars such as WW2 with ideas such as air-support. Germany only ever built 21 tanks so it wasn't until the Second Battle of Villers-Bretonneux that saw first ever tank on tank battle when the Germans brought 14 of their tanks to the front. The ground-breaking battle involved 3 British tanks against 3 German tanks which arguably resulted in a win for the British.

Major-General Fuller planned to use a huge number of tanks to attack Germany in 1919 if the war had lasted that long and his plans were the basis for the famous Blitzkrieg tactics of Germany in WW2.

15 DESERT CAMPAIGNS

So much of the history of The Great War concentrates on the battles of Europe that it is easy to forget that it is called a World War for a reason; its participants were scattered widely and its theatre of campaigns took place around the globe. One of sometimes forgotten areas of conflict was in the Middle-East; it not only gave us one of the great iconic figures of the war but also had repercussions which are with us to the present day.

Traditionally the Middle-East had long been the playground of the Ottoman Empire, based out of Istanbul and the Safavids from Iran. Eventually the Turks came out on top and their empire stretched from the gates of Vienna to Egypt and Arabia. However, it was only a matter of time before technology and innovation allowed first the Portuguese and then the French to get footholds in the region before Great Britain took over areas of the Persian Gulf and Egypt.

The Young Turks tried to reform their grand old empire but it was too little, too late and by WW1, the Ottomans were well on their way out. The Middle-East campaigns are important for several reasons including the ideas of Nationalism which were giving Arabs hopes for independence and because Britain was anxious both not to loose control of the Suez Canal and its links with India. More immediately Great Britain wanted to inflict as great a territorial loss over the Ottomans as possible following the Turks joining the Axis powers at the start of the war.

The British were also concerned that the Axis powers would gain access to oil, particularly in southern Iran and they were assisted in their actions against the Ottomans by Russia who had been gradually conquering Ottomans lands in the preceding century or so and had the goal of destroying the Ottomans and claiming Istanbul as its own. The Ottomans made the initial mistake of sending 90,000 men to Romania in support of its allies which greatly reduced its ability to defend its Islamic heartlands whilst

Russia drew on the support of 20,000 Armenians ready to revolt for their freedom and Britain had a deployment of Indian troops in neighbouring Iran.

The war started with the Ottomans heavily reliant on German equipment, training and in some cases officers. They joined with Germany with bombing the Russian port of Odessa. In November 1914, the Russian crossed the border with aims of capturing the key eastern Ottoman city of Dogubeyzit whilst a few weeks later the British captured the Iraqi second city of Basra from Turkish forces.

January 1915 saw the British make inroads into Iraq despite efforts by Ottoman naval forces which were seen off by the Royal Navy and then Ottoman efforts to capture the Suez Canal also failed. Pleased with the progress made so far Sir John Nixon ordered British forces to take a more aggressive posture and advance into Iraq with the possible aim of capturing Iraq. The Ottomans were in disarray with changes in command and ineffectual attacks by Arab allies until in the end a German General was brought in to take command of the defence of Baghdad. Even more worryingly the Allied landings at Gallipoli brought the war within a few miles of Istanbul itself.

Throughout 1915, British and Indian forces made good progress through Iraq and as they did so, they gained the support of local Arab tribes who were keen to support the winning side though whether the British supported their massacres of hospitalised Ottoman troop at Amara is doubtful. At the Battle of Ctesiphon, just south of Baghdad, the British and Ottomans fought a five day battle to a standstill with the result that both sides retreated. However the Ottoman commander noticing his enemy were retreating turned around and instead gave chase until the British fortified their position at Ku-Al-Amara. The Ottomans laid siege as well as sending further forces downstream to cut off any attempts at re-enforcing and the British.

In hindsight, the British should have continued back to Basra where they could be easily re-supplied but as it happened three attempts were made to break the siege and all failed with heavy casualties on both sides. The British expeditionary force was under siege from 7th December 1915 and under new leadership the Ottoman force gave the option of starving or surrendering with only very limited supplies dropped by air. The conditions in the British camp were appalling, many men died of dysentery, typhoid and cholera. Britain entered into secret negotiations to pay huge amounts of money to let the force go free under the promise Britain would freeze its war with the Ottomans but the request was turned down. When a final attempt to break the siege by river steamer failed, on 29th April 1916 the British command surrendered and over 13,000 men were taken prisoner and marched off to internment in Syria.

Realising their huge setback was due to a lack of logistical infrastructure, the British spent the next year improving their situation until when Ottoman forces were overly concerned by possible Russian movements in the north, the British finally entered Baghdad on 11th March 1917 after devastating the Ottoman defending forces. By the end of the war, over 350,000 British and often largely Indian forces had fought in the area with 92,000 deaths.

Meanwhile in Arabia in 1916, the Arabs revolted from their Ottoman overlords under the auspices of Prince Feisal and under advisement of a small group of British officers. By far the most well-known of these is T.E. Lawrence, better known to many as Lawrence of Arabia and his fame is such that he was the one Allied soldier who not only rivalled but surpassed the glory of the Red Baron. Thomas Edward Lawrence was born on 16th August 1889. Born illegitimate did not stop Lawrence in these times of high moral values and he still managed to enter Oxford University and graduate with First Class honours, taking up an interest in archaeology and working in the Middle-East even before WW1. This gave him valuable experience of travelling through the Ottoman provinces.

When war arrived the Ottomans had only a tenuous grip on Arabia and used its train network which connected the important cities of Mecca and Medina with Amman, Jerusalem and Damascus. Devised by the British Arab Bureau and enacted by Lawrence, they drew up a plan on the basis that they knew the Ottomans would stop at nothing to preserve their control and so diverting resources from other areas of the war. In October 1916 Lawrence was sent to the Hejaz in Arabia and worked with Prince Feisal amongst others to create an irregular force composed of individual Arab tribes that all sought freedom from the Turks. The fact that Prince Feisal was the son of Sherif Hussein of Mecca was a useful recruitment inducement and this resulting army used the natural ability of the Arab tribes to travel across the desert, attacking isolated Ottoman positions and blowing up train lines, destroying Ottoman communication and transportation networks before disappearing quickly and quietly into the desert where they would be next to impossible to follow. It was a policy that we would know today as Asymmetric Warfare.

The tactics that Lawrence oversaw was successful not just militarily in seizing objectives and disrupting communications but also compelling the Ottomans to expend much additional manpower that ideally would have been much more effectively used against regular British forces. Fresh from initial success and more significant military support from the Royal Navy and British Army, Lawrence succeeded in forming an alliance with Auda Abu Tay who until then had been an Ottoman ally and the newly enlarged force took the strategic Ottoman positions at 'Aqaba.

The Ottomans made a second effort to capture the Suez Canal and when they failed, the British chased them back towards Palestine until they were held up by the fort at Gaza. With the arrival of General Allenby and large re-enforcements, the British at last captured Gaza and just before Christmas entered Jerusalem, which, was not only a huge morale boost but obviously along with various political documents, paved the way for the later creation of the state of Israel.

After a delay caused by a renewed German offensive in Europe, the British were able to make a concerted attack on the Ottoman forces and defeated them both in set piece battles and hit and run attacks by Lawrence and his forces. Lawrence became both a British hero but also a hero to the Arab world. He received numerous promotions and won the Distinguished Service order in the British Army whilst he was given a status equal to the sons of the Sherif of Mecca in Arabia. This high status and the simple love the Arab people had for Lawrence meant that the huge £15,000 bounty the Ottomans placed on him went without any takers.

With General Allenby moving up the Mediterranean coast, Lawrence's forces moved north and Damascus was captured in the autumn of 1918. The Ottoman Empire was forced to enter peace talks leaving it with just a rump of territory which was only as big as it was due to the early Russian withdrawal from the war and a resulting separate treaty which saw the Russians hand back some of their conquests.

Lawrence of Arabia achieved worldwide fame thanks in part to his relation with the American journalist Lowell Thomas who reported in depth on the Middle-East campaign. After failing to keep the Arab lands free from French and British protection, Lawrence fell back into his naturally reclusive state, which is part of the reason he loved the desert so much due to the anonymity it gave him. After advising the British government in the post-war conferences and surviving a plane crash in Egypt that killed others, he returned to England as a Colonel but soon joined the RAF under an assumed name and a lowly rank serving in the U.K. and India and also for a time in the Royal Tank Corps. Sadly he died aged just 46 when involved in a motorcycle accident close to his Dorset home and was buried nearby at a funeral attended by such names as Sir Winston Churchill. His death was such a shock that it went someway towards the development of motorcycle helmets.

The Sykes-Picot agreement had one of the longest standing impacts on the world by partitioning the Middle-East up into British and French zones and creating artificial states albeit sometimes based upon historical or ethnic divisions. For those wanting to understand the problems in Iraq, Syria or the Israel-

Palestinian problem then it all goes back to the agreement that Lawrence fought so hard to avoid enacting.

16 WAR IN THE AIR

Though there had been limited use of balloons in areas of reconnaissance and to assist with artillery shelling, The Great War was the first that actually used airborne devices as a method of attacking the enemy, in effect opening a new theatre of war.

Though there were more than a few doubts about the use of powered aircraft in war, the British used aerial reconnaissance to immediately save around 100,000 men when it was revealed that they were going to be surrounded by a German force and that they should withdraw. Part of the success of the First Battle of Marne was due to reconnaissance information detailing weak spots in the German lines.

To a great degree it was the French who set the lead with powered aircraft with Great Britain catching up whilst the United States still had hardly any aircraft of note even in 1917. The Germans had been preoccupied with Zeppelins as at first it wasn't clear that aircraft would be the superior technology. Zeppelins could also carry a far bigger bomb payload and the Kaiser authorised their use in the war providing they avoid London and other civilian areas.

The first Zeppelin raid took place on the night of the 19-20th January 1915 and though their original target was the docks and industrial areas around Humberside, strong winds blew the Zeppelins off course and they ended up bombing Kings Lynn, Sheringham and Great Yarmouth on the Norfolk coast, killing 4 people and injuring 16 more. May 1915 saw further bombing raids on Ipswich, Southend, Ramsgate and Dover. On May 31st East London had 120 bombs dropped costing 7 lives and injuring 35 more.

As attempts to intercept and shoot down Zeppelins were totally ineffectual, a blackout was imposed and the London press did not publicise the bombed locations so as to not assist German navigation. June saw serious damage caused to Hull as well as some success when a German Zeppelin raid ran into a British attack which saw one German vessel destroyed on the ground and another destroyed in mid-air when Reginald Warneford dropped six bombs onto it, an action that saw him award the Victoria Cross.

The rest of 1915 saw further Zeppelin attacks on Tyneside and London with their main effects being to cause terror amongst the civilians of Britain. Further attacks in the autumn killed over 100, mostly in and around London.

Advances were made in anti-Zeppelin guns with a new type of explosive charge used and the ability to fire at targets at higher altitude but still 1916 saw 293 people killed and 691 injured along the East-Coast, London and industrial cities such as Liverpool and further bombing raids were made in the final two years of the war as an arms race developed between the British defenders and the Zeppelins that were becoming, bigger, more powerful and flying at higher altitudes (24,900feet). However, the focus of the war in the air was shifting to the aeroplane and the last Zeppelin raid that was targeting Northern England was shot down over the North Sea with its crew being burned alive. Nevertheless nearly 6,000 Zeppelin bombs killed 557 people and injured 1,358 more. Whilst the raids caused £1.5 million of damage, even more costly was the diverted resources and the lost production of great chunks of wartime munitions.

Flying aircraft in WW1 was a particularly dangerous task with even reconnaissance pilots having a life span of hours, let alone combat pilots. Early bombing raids by planes did take place but they carried a much smaller payload than Zeppelins and they were also hindered by a lack of basic technology such as bombsights. The first air to air combat was a case of one Russian pilot ramming an Austrian and then things developed to pilots shooting passing planes with pistols but this was both an inaccurate and ineffective way of bringing down planes. On October 5th 1914, Louis Quenault fitted a machine gun to his plane and things got more serious. At first there was a huge risk of pilots shooting themselves out of the sky should their machine gun bullets hit their own propellers. The French put bullet-proof deflectors on their propellers but even so bullets could end up bouncing off them and hitting the pilot who fired them. It was the development of the synchronised machine gun that would only fire bullets in the spaces between the moving propellers that meant that air-combat became a deadly arena and it was the Germans that developed it first.

The second half of 1915 saw what was referred to as The Fokker Scourge as the German Fokker monoplane (i.e. not a bi-plane or tri-plane which until this time were the mainstay of powered aircraft) had a large technical advantage against Allied aircraft and was responsible for a large number of downed British and French planes. Fokkers were also the first to start using metal in the plane fuselage as previously planes had been made out of wood, wire and a stretched canvas like material. In these times, WW1 pilots were seen as chivalrous and glamorous, rather like modern-day knights and non more so than German hotshot Max Immelman who led his own team of flyers at the time known as a circus and who was such a great pilot, he invented several manoeuvres of aerial warfare including the Immelman turn which are still studied by pilots today. The period of German dominance only ended in the spring of 1916 when the French developed a superior plane and the British changed their tactics and began flying in groups

Technology was moving so quickly that each new model of plane was quickly outdated with both the Allies and Central Powers swapping periods of dominance. Though now not as well remembered as Spitfires, Hurricanes and Lancasters, WW1 saw a number of legendary planes including the Fokker, Nieuport, Albatross, Sopwith Camel and Spad.

Pilots went into battle woefully under-trained, and few bothered to help or get to know the new pilots as their life expectancy was so short, often only a day or two. Nevertheless, tactics improved and developed and the British started using aircraft to strafe trenches, as if the poor fellows on the ground didn't have it hard enough already. Germany began to produce bomber squadrons and others that concentrated on attacked British ground positions.

The first half of 1917 was very much one where Germany enjoyed air-superiority with its well-armed Albatross DIII planes with the Royal Flying Corps, the precursor to the RAF, suffering heavy losses. These culminated in the 'Bloody April' of 1917 when the RFC lost 245 planes with 211 crew killed and another 108 captured. Many of these losses were due to the work of Jasta 11, a fighter squadron led by the legendary Baron Von Richthofen, a fighter ace, who in all made 80 kills. He was known as the Red Baron as his plane was painted bright red. His entire squadron was manned by extraordinary pilots and meeting up with them combined with their superior planes usually had just one result.

One of those killed by the Red Baron in Bloody April was a relation of the author, Serjeant Reuel Dunn, who was a gunner. His Sopwith 1 ½ Stutter plane piloted by Lt Peter Warren had shot down three German planes by 2nd April 1917 and had completed a mission taking vital aerial photography of German defensive positions just east of Vimy Ridge when they were flying back to base and were attacked by the Red Baron and two of his fellow hot-shots. Dunn's plane was split off from the rest of its squadron and had its petrol tank shot through. It tried to evade its pursuers by flying into a bank of cloud but Von Richthofen continued to attack and the plane was forced to land just 300 yards east of Givenchy. Normally chivalry would take over and the German would have continued on his way but Serjeant Dunn didn't look for an easy way out and instead even though he was a sitting duck, opened fired on the Red Baron and badly damaged his plane forcing the Red Baron to attack once more. Serjeant Dunn was fatally wounded with machine gun bullets lodged in his stomach, whilst Lt. Warren who had bullet holes in his trousers and shirt sleeves was totally unhurt and taken prisoner. The Red Baron was so impressed that he visited Reuel Dunn in hospital that evening meeting him shortly before he died.

By the summer of 1917, a new generation of British fighters reached the Western Front and Germany never again had such air superiority. The Red Baron went on to become a national hero in Germany as his flying circus devastated the Royal Flying Corps but he too was destined to not make it through the war and he was shot down and killed near Amiens on 21st April 1918. He had been on the attack when he too came briefly under fire from Canadian Captain Arthur "Roy" Brown and was shot through the heart and lungs. However, tests conducted almost a century later indicate that he was actually killed by a 'lucky' shot from ground troops. He managed to make a very rough landing and died moments after Australian soldiers reached his plane with his last word supposedly being "Kaputt". The most successful British pilot, Major Edward Mannock VC with 73 kills on hearing of his death proclaimed that he "hoped he bastard burnt all the way down", however he was given a full military funeral with a commemoration of 'to our gallant and worthy foe'.

17 GALLIPOLI

The Gallipoli campaign in the Dardanelles region of modern day Turkey was a landmark battle of World War One. It is counted as perhaps the greatest Ottoman Turkish victory in the war and set about creating a Turkish nationalism that went on to create a modern country out of the ashes of defeat at the end of the war. Gallipoli is also pivotal in the creation of a modern national consciousness for Australia and New Zealand, separate to that with its historic links with the United Kingdom but for altogether more tragic reasons.

Gallipoli sits on the Dardanelles Straits which linked the Mediterranean to the Black Sea and which could have linked the Royal Navy with the Russian Navy if only the Dardanelles were not just controlled by the Ottomans but only a short distance from their capital, Istanbul.

By the end of 1914, the Western Front was already at stalemate and there was no overland trade route between Western Europe and Russia and so a plan was drawn up to capture the Dardanelle Straits which would not just open up the seaways for the Allies but possibly lead to a quick capture Istanbul, putting the Ottoman Empire out of the war before it had barely begun.

The 17th February 1915 saw a British seaplane from HMS Ark Royal followed by a huge bombardment two days later by a powerful joint British-French force headed up by the Battleship HMS Queen Elizabeth, which began bombarding and ultimately destroying many of the outlying forts and a detachment of Royal Marines even landed to blow up Ottoman artillery. However bad weather and a mobile Ottoman military, frustrated the Allies from being able to complete their task.

The 18th March saw a large attack composed of no less than 18 Battleships and aided by a number of destroyers and cruisers bombarded the coasts as mine-sweepers attempted to clear the straits but a number of important ships were damaged by a new and unknown minefield which had only been laid a few days earlier. Despite many British officers believing they were close to victory on account that the few remaining Ottoman artillery posts were low on ammunition, the order was given to withdraw and instead attempts to secure the straits fell to the land forces.

At this point 78,000 Australian and New Zealand soldiers were undergoing training in Egypt in preparation for deployment to the Western Front but with the focus on Gallipoli, these men were put in the newly created Australian and New Zealand Army Corps (ANZAC). The men had not trained for making a landing under fire and it was not thought that the Ottoman defenders would put up much of a fight but both turned out to be terrible mistakes.

The Ottomans under Kemal Attaturk and with the assistance of German officers had prepared a robust defence especially as the Allies invasion of the 23rd April was pushed back two days due to bad conditions. Six beaches were chosen for the landings composed of British, French and Anzac groups followed shortly afterwards by Indian troops. Only 10% of the British soldiers at 'V' Beach made it ashore due to heavy machine-gun fire and similar events took place at what would be known as Anzac Cove where Ottoman defenders stopped any potential invasion either on or just above the beach and who held fortified positions with good vantage points on the Allied soldiers below. On W Beach, the Lancashires lost 600 of their 1,000 men but still managed to take the Ottoman positions whilst of over 1,000 Irish troops only 11 were to get through the campaign unscathed.

The Allied attack stalled because of the slaughter on the beaches and the fact that those positions that managed to get off the beach didn't push onwards and maximise their advantages. This allowed ample time for the Ottomans to rush in re-enforcements although an Australian submarine did manage to get through the minefield and cause panic amongst Ottoman shipping.

April 27th saw 12 Ottoman Battalion reinforcements arrive but still the Allies pushed forward, assisted greatly by the naval bombardment but eventually the advance was halted and like elsewhere the landings turned into a long drawn out war of attrition. Allied ships were successful at the nearby Sea of Marmara and several Ottoman ships were lost including the Gul Djemal, which was carrying 6,000 men and a field battery in reinforcements.

The 5th May saw the Allies launch a major attack and they made a few hundred metres before heavy fire from the Ottomans eventually caused the whole plan to be abandoned on the 7th May and both sides consolidated their positions with the Ottomans using their superior position to pick off men and officers with sniper fire.

On May 19th the Ottomans launched a 42,000 strong counter-attack with the aim of driving the Anzacs into the sea, their surprise attack ruined when they were spotted by British reconnaissance aircraft resulting in them suffering 3,000 men killed and more than four times that injured. Only 160 Anzacs were killed but one of them was a stretcher bearer named John Simpson Kirkpatrick who evacuated wounded men on the back of donkey. His story quickly became the stuff of legends amongst the Australian forces and in Australia generally. Such were the heavy Ottoman losses that the Anzacs agreed to a truce to allow the Ottomans to recover their dead which allowed men from both sides to mingle in a similar manner to the famous Christmas truce on the Western Front.

Though the British ship HMS Goliath was torpedoed which greatly affected their ability to launch effective onshore bombardments, HMS E11 managed to pass through the Dardanelles and disabled or sank 11 enemy vessels and even reached Constantinople harbour itself where it damaged a gunboat and the harbour side which saw its Captain Martin Nasmith awarded a Victoria Cross, just one of many in the Gallipoli campaign.

Due to the lack of heavy artillery and an unwillingness to repeat the slaughter of their last major attack against the Anzacs, the Ottomans became unwilling to mount further frontal assaults and instead saw increased use of tunnelling.

June and July saw more of the same with the both sides seeing casualty rates of around 25%. The Allies seemed unable to make inroads whilst the Ottomans couldn't push them back into the sea with the Divisional strength of both sides increasing from 5 and 6 to 15 and 16 respectively. The stalemate forced the Allies to come up with a new plan to capture the high ground with two new divisions landing 5 miles north of Anzac Cove at Suvla Bay on August 6th whilst a renewed attempt on the high ground at Sari Blair would be made by existing troops. The landing was successful but the Ottomans on the high ground stopped the Allied force really getting off the beach despite successful Australian diversion attacks nearby.

New Zealand forces managed to get within 500 metres of their objective without actually making it and nearby Australian and Indian groups actually got lost in the dark and were easily seen off by the Ottoman defenders.

Back in Europe Lord Kitchener decided it was time to make a big push in France which meant there were only limited men left to reinforce the troops at Gallipoli and with Bulgaria now entering the war it meant the Ottomans could more easily get substantial German reinforcements. On 25th September Kitchener ordered that 3 Divisions leave the Dardanelles for Salonika in Greece.

The summer heat affected both sides with many succumbing to outbreaks of disease and both sides suffering from supply problems leading to ordinary men to strike up conversation and bartering with their opponents. In the autumn, it was a different story with the Allied troops in their poor positions being deluged by three days of rain and then snow, and so it was decided that the Allies withdraw from Gallipoli, leaving their flooded trenches and unburied dead where they were. Most troops were recovered in an orderly fashion throughout December with the last men leaving on 8th January 1916. Allied vehicles were sabotaged and over 500 mules were killed to prevent them falling into Ottoman hands.

The Gallipoli campaign is often looked at as an unmitigated disaster and while the Allies didn't come close to meeting their objectives they did succeed in using up vast amount of Ottoman resources. The Allies suffered from bad planning, poor logistics, inaccurate maps and intelligence and undefined goals whilst the Turks held onto all the high and most defensive positions. Additionally, Allied submarines had all but stopped the Ottoman navy from venturing out to sea with all the supply problems this created.

Some of the Anzac officers were promoted after the campaign whilst Gallipoli was at last the undoing of Lord Kitchener with the new coalition government quickly losing faith in him. Meanwhile the Ottoman successes inspired their men in future actions against the British in the Middle-East, notably in Iraq.

However there can be no doubt that the Gallipoli campaign was a disaster for Allied morale and the mistakes made went on to influence much more successful amphibious landings at D-Day, the Pacific WW2 campaign and more recently the incredible British landings at the Falklands in 1982.

Anzac Day is now remembered in Australia and New Zealand annually on the 25th April to commemorate the over 11,000 dead out of their force of 35,000. However it wasn't just the Anzacs that suffered as the Ottomans lost over 56,000, the British 34,000 and France nearly 10,000. British Indian and Newfoundland forces also suffered high casualty rates.

18 WW1 URBAN LEGENDS

In any war, facts are muddled, eye witness accounts confused or forgotten all too easily in the horrors of war. Few wars can come close to The Great War in its potential for misunderstandings and unbelievable yet established feats of heroism. Related to these are two stories related to the war that quickly gained almost mythical status amongst the Allies and also some Germans but did the either the Crucified Soldier or The Angel of Mons actually occur?

Within weeks of the war starting there was a widespread and much-believed report that an Angel or Angels had saved the British whilst retreating under pressure from a vastly superior German force after the Battle of Mons in August 1914.

Those looking for more Earthly reasons for the events that took place after the first major British battle of WW1 might opt for the fact that the British Expeditionary Force were beaten and exhausted and forced to march through the 5 days and nights, exhausted and prone to hallucinations possibly inspired by the published story "The Bowmen" where British forces were assisted by St George and a force of supernatural medieval bowmen.

Nevertheless, the reports of divine intervention did nothing but spread with numerous men and officers swearing as to what they saw and this was used to assure a scared population back at home that Britain was fighting on the side of good against the evil of Germany. Surprisingly though the stories of Angelic protection occurred months after publication of "The Bowmen" with some stating the reports were encouraged as part of an official war policy.

However, there is some correspondence from soldiers at the Front that predate the publication of "The Bowmen" and still make mention of the miracle of the British force being protected by Angels. One veteran is reported to have been a hard drinking man until he saw the Angels and from then on changed his life, quit drinking for ever and after the war became a pillar of his community. Additionally, the weather reports that afternoon as being hot and sunny with no clouds whatsoever.

It is easy today for people to disbelieve such reports but at the time, they were reported by respectable figures in the military and in some cases even verified by German soldiers. Whether it was tiredness, unusual cloud formations, supernatural forces or actual Angels, the one thing that all versions of the story can agree on is that something strange occurred that afternoon and the British forces made an unlikely escape from an overwhelming German army.

The story of the Crucified Soldier on the Western Front is another one of the legendary elements of The Great War that almost immediately took the nation and world by storm. For a while it was accepted unquestionably and then for several decades it was thought perhaps to be some Allied propaganda to illustrate the depravity of the German soldiers in the Western Front. Recent research however seems to indicate that this awful story has more than a touch of truth about it.

The account of the Crucified Soldier came from three witnesses that state they saw a Canadian soldier crucified by bayonets to a barn door near the town of Ypres 24th April 1915. However the report was non-conclusive with no body being recovered and certain differences in their accounts. It all came to light in a report in The Times on 10th May 1915 when it was reported that a group of Canadians stated their officer had been crucified to a wall by having bayonets pushed through his hands and feet and finally his throat before he was shot.

Within days the reports had reached the House of Commons and a few days later it was reported that the officer was in fact a sergeant and that figure of Christ had been removed from a village cross and the unfortunate Canadian crucified alive took his place.

Various accounts appeared, some of them obviously factually

incorrect including one where a Canadian soldier in the medical corps had been identified as the crucified man only for the soldier to write in to the paper claiming it was most definitely not him! Other reports surfaced where the crucified soldier was British rather than Canadian and with such variations in the story despite being used effectively for worldwide propaganda there was no concrete evidence for any crucifixion.

This changed in 2002 when a Channel 4 documentary maker by the name of Iain Overton investigated all of the accounts thoroughly in a scientific and systematic fashion. He uncovered new evidence that led him to believe that the story of the Crucified Soldier wasn't an urban myth but actually a reality. The unfortunate soldier was Sergeant Harry Band of the Central Ontario Regiment of the Canadian Infantry, who was reported missing in action on 24 April 1915 near Ypres. His body was never recovered and a number of letters sent to his sister by his comrade's state that sadly he was the crucified soldier. Other evidence included a contemporary typed note by a nurse stating that a Sergeant Band had been crucified by 5 bayonets against the doors of a barn.

19 THEY CALLED IT PASSCHENDAELE

Passchendaele is another of one of the epic battles that shook the western front between the British and Allied soldiers against the Germans. It all took place on the low ridges to the south and east of Ypres, in the Belgian region of Flanders between July and November 1917. British High Command hoped to take the vital railway junctions at Rosslare, only 5 miles away but it was an objective that would go unmet until 1918. Though the Battle of Passchendaele is a distinct event in itself, it was just part of the wider and endless conflict in the area as evident by its alternative name the Third Battle of Ypres.

The conditions at Passchendaele were nothing short of an abomination and with hundreds of thousands dead on both sides. It is a name that sends shivers down the spines of anyone who knows anything about WW1 not because of the casualties which it took for Britain to narrowly win a strategic victory but primarily due to the awful conditions that the battle took place in.

The terrain in this section of the Western Front that even a very modest hill of a few dozen feet became tactical strongholds that were fiercely fought over. The slight elevation, no matter how slight, was still relatively higher than the surrounding land which meant it was more defendable, allowed observation of the enemy and particularly in trench warfare, was less likely to get bogged down.

Passchendaele was a controversial campaign from the off as British Prime Minister David Lloyd George didn't agree with it and didn't even approve it. The decision to proceed with it was down to the much aligned and often rightly so, Field Marshall Sir Douglas Haig, who was anxious to make the attack, unwilling to wait for the looming American re-enforcements.

Haig though believed the Germans were worn out and yet couldn't refuse to fight here as it would make their surrounding front line untenable following the recent Allied victory at Messines Ridge. The Germans themselves knew that they were in a tough situation and opinion amongst German High Command was divided over whether they should retreat their forces slightly further east.

On July 31st 1917, British forces launched an attack known as the Battle of Pilckem Ridge. Though their attack was hindered by dense low cloud, they pushed the Germans back by around 3,700 metres before the Germans counter-attacked from the sides which pushed the British a long way back towards the starting point before the Germans too were fought to a standstill courtesy of machine gun fire and heavy mud. The British had suffered 70% casualties in the battle.

Early August saw the British capture Westhoek though at some cost in lives whilst the Canadians assaulted and captured Hill 70 and incurred a costly defeat on the Germans which meant German plans were wrecked for relieving their 'fought out' forces in Flanders. Other smaller battles were fought throughout August with British advances often being small and temporary for the loss of many men.

Things weren't going to plan and many British and other Allied resources were diverted to fight in Italy, the German forces remain doggedly resistant but perhaps worst of all was the weather.

The soil type at Passchendaele is different to the sandy composition at Ypres or the balanced soil at the nearby Messines Ridge and is instead similar to London Clay. Allied Intelligence knew the area before the war to be well drained but for some reason unbeknownst to them, most of the drains and streams in the area had been destroyed by the war meaning that only a small amount of rain would lead to a wet, sticky and boggy surface. The problem was that the Battle of Passchendaele just happened to take place during the wettest summer that Passchendaele had suffered in years and the washout summer soon turned into a washout autumn and an early winter.

Duckboards were laid out and accidentally stepping off one was a major disaster for the individuals involved. Horses unlucky enough to step in the mud would soon be forever lost in a swamp of water, mud and craters. A British officer recalled seeing a man who had accidentally fallen off the duckboard and had become stuck up to his knees in a shell-hole. The man couldn't get out himself and his friends tried relentlessly to pull him out but failed and they couldn't dare walk out and get him as they too would be well and truly stuck. Two days later the officer passed by again and was alarmed to see that the stuck man had now sank up to his neck in mud, his exhausted friends forced to abandon him, he had gone completely mad.

The weather improved in September and the British were no longer fighting both the enemy and the conditions. The Germans were forced to change their defensive deployments and every machine gun that could be found was brought up to the front line and orders were issued for gas attacks to be made at every opportunity. The British too were reinforced particularly by big gun artillery and as the British advances had been relatively modest, they had taken time to dig in meaning that German attacks had little effect. Not that they didn't try as between 26th September and the 3rd October the Germans made 24 attacks.

The 20th-25th September saw the Battle of Menin Road Ridge where the British used their new artillery to destroy German machine gun nests and concrete pillar boxes and there was an increase in the use of Aircraft to observe on German movements. By mid-morning on the 20th, the British had pushed the Germans back about a mile over a wide section of the front and though the 25th saw the Germans retake some positions despite heavy casualties, they were entirely swept away the next day in the Battle of Polygon Wood.

October saw further bad news for the Germans as the British continued to make small and occasional tangent advances but the losses they inflicted on Germany was severe. British artillery was for a time almost unanswered and eventually senior German officers were planning to make an orderly retreat from the Ypres salient despite the terrible casualties they had taken to win and keep it for so many years and regardless of the fact it would leave German forces to the north compromised right up to the Belgian coast.

The 12th October saw an attempt to advance again but the terrible weather and mud hampered operations. The Allied soldiers were thoroughly exhausted and understandably suffering from low morale and a German counter-attack pushed the Allies back with over 13,000 casualties with New Zealand suffering their worst day in their military history.

Bad weather in October meant that British advances stalled in the mud until supply roads were strengthened allowing the heavy artillery and after repeated British requests, the French fought an overwhelming victory at La Mamaison taking over 11,000 German prisoners.

Despite all of this, the front line in the area was pretty much the same as it had been in April 1915. A series of small-scale assaults continued at the end of October before the rain, at last, paused for a few days allowing the Allies to prepare to attack the village of Passchendaele itself and on 6th November Canadian troops finally occupied the village just 3 hours after launching their attack and when they occupied Hill 52 just to the north of Passchendaele the tragic muddled battle had finally come to an end.

The Battle of Passchendaele was condemned by both sides. PM Lloyd George wrote that it was one of the most senseless battles of the war and totally indefensible whilst the German High Command believed that the battle had brought Germany to her knees and faced almost certain destruction

20 THE WAR AROUND THE WORLD

Though this book concentrates on the main theatres of war, there are other areas that also saw a great deal of combat in the First World War.

Serbian Campaign

With the outbreak of war, Austro-Hungary had a huge army of 414,000 with a further mobilisation of over 4 million men which allowed 200,000 new troops to arrive at the front each month. With such strong forces, the Austro-Hungarian Empire as expected, invaded Serbia after beating the Serbian army in two initial battles. The Austro-Hungary army wasn't of a good quality, and many of its men were conscripted from around the empire and unable to speak German or Hungarian.

It is one of the great fight backs of modern warfare that the Serbians with an army only half the size of the Austro-Hungarian forces at most, managed a stark turnaround in the fortunes of Serbia which managed to repulse the invasion and so ended the hope of the Central Powers that the conflict would be a short one. Serbia was constantly plagued by a lack of manpower and of equipment It took several months for large consignments of rifles to arrive from the Allies but it was saved to some degree by the large Russian forces who by necessity diverted many of the men and resources of the Austro-Hungary forces away from Serbia to the Eastern Front. Still the fighting was fierce with almost 400,000 men being killed between the two sides by Christmas 1914.

When the Ottomans suffered defeats throughout much of 1915, a renewed Austro-Hungary effort to conquer Serbia was put in place with the view of connecting Germany with Turkey by railway to ease the supply routes. To make things worse for Serbia, the Central Powers persuaded Bulgaria to attack Serbia and keep any land that they conquered.

In October 1915, Serbia was attacked by Bulgarian, Austro-Hungarian and German armies on separate fronts and despite putting up a strong resistance, and had to retreat to the Adriatic Coast to be rescued by British and French shipping. There was such fierce fighting and such a long and weary retreat that many Serbs died from exhaustion for weeks after they were rescued and indeed their leader Marshal Putnik had to be carried away from the front line never recovered and died over a year later in France.

A British and French forced left Thessalonica in Greece and diverted much of the Bulgarian forces away from Serbia but was forced to retreat by December 1915 leaving Montenegro to stand and fall in January 1916 against the Austro-Hungary forces. All in all it had been a total and decisive victory for the Central Powers and allowed the tactical rail link between Germany and Istanbul as had been planned.

A Serbian uprising was put down in the spring of 1917 but gradually a mainly Franco/Serbian force managed to make inroads in Macedonia with British and Greek forces again pushing forward from Thessalonica. Bulgaria saw its only major defeat of the war at the Battle of Dobro Pole on 15th September 1918 which left it compelled to seek surrender and only narrowly avoided being occupied by the Entente Powers. This opened the way for Serbia to be liberated and the long road to Vienna was open with the Bulgarian Army now out of the equation. As such the Austro-Hungarians were forced to the peace table.

It is hard to imagine the terrible losses that Serbia suffered during the war with 1.1 million dying out of a total population of 4.5 million and many of these were civilian deaths caused by food shortages and disease epidemics. The lost Serbian generation is something that has affected the country ever since.

Romania was one of those countries that saw a great deal of fighting in WW1. They had been allied to the Austro-Hungarian Empire for nearly 30 years before the war started but the Romanian government argued that they weren't bound to support the Central Powers as it was Austria that started the war.

With the promise of territorial transfers if they entered the war on the side of the Allies, Romania entered the war relatively late in August 1916. Romania hoped to conquer Transylvania and with the assistance of Russia fought solidly but were eventually pushed back and when the Russian Revolution took the Russians out of the war. Romania was all but surrounded and forced to sue for peace on 9th December 1917 at Focsani with much of the country falling under occupation.

Romania nominally re-entered the war for one day on November 10th 1918 and the Treaty of Versailles superseded the punitive measures of the Focsani treaty. An estimated 220,000 Romanians died fighting for the Allied cause which represents about 6% of the Entente/Allied death-toll.

African Theatre

One of the primary reasons behind The Great War was that Germany longed to have an empire of equal standing to Great Britain and France and in the preceding decades had been occupying chunks of Africa not yet claimed by The Great Powers. World War One however was going to have the precise opposite effect and the Scramble for Africa ended with the German colonies being divided amongst the Allies.

The Berlin Treaty of 1884 stated that all African colonies were to be neutral in the event of war in Europe and, as a result, they weren't heavily guarded. Nevertheless war came to Africa almost immediately as Britain decided that German outposts were a threat to its control of the global sea-lanes and so in 1914 the Kings African Rifles attacked the numerically superior German force in East Africa with battle raging throughout the war until 1917. As the war progressed Britain brought in re-enforcements from across the Empire, particularly from India and the Belgians also played a significant role.

World War One in Africa wasn't simply a war between European states, there were also native Africans who saw the war as an opportunity to rebel and possibly win their freedom. A major revolt occurred in Malawi against an unduly strict local British official. The revolt was put down but it did result in local political and social reforms that improved the welfare for the local indigenous people.

There were several military campaigns in North Africa during WW1. France expended a great deal of effort fighting the Zaian confederation of Berber tribes in and around Morocco, these tribes having been financed by the Central Powers to stir up discontent and rebellion. Further east in

Libya, British forces fought the Senussi Campaign against Ottoman and German-backed forces which the Ottomans hoped would threaten the Suez Canal from the west as well as enticing a Jihad amongst Egyptians. The Jihad never materialised and after 15 months of fighting, the British were victorious in Libya despite an attempt by the Sultan of Darfur in modern day Sudan to co-ordinate a campaign against the British at the same time.

In West Africa, British forces invaded Togoland on 7th August 1914 and with French support from neighbouring colonies they overcame tough German resistance but quickly and easily won through with the German colony surrendering on August 26th 1914.

A much longer campaign took place in the German colony of Cameroon. Whilst the British were successful against the Germans of the Tepe, the British commander Colonel Maclear was ordered to capture the northern German fort at Mora but were unable to and instead placed it under a siege that lasted for the duration of the war. In the south of the country British forces were heavily defeated at the Battle of Nsanakong.

In 1915, the Germans repositioned themselves to a more mountainous area near Jaunde and a German force mounted an invasion of Nigeria whilst later in the year the British began make progress in a series of small battles although they were hindered by bad weather. When the British captured a German fort at the Battle of Banjo on 6th November, the writing was on the wall for the Germans as the British along with French and Belgian re-enforcements converged on the German stronghold near Jaunde. In December 1915, the German commander Carl Zimmerman ordered the Germany army and civilians to flee into the Spanish colony of Riu Muni which eventually saw over 10,000 escape capture by the Allies with many being shipped out to other German forces.

Down in Southwest Africa on 25th September 1914, the Battle of Sandfontein saw German forces take the initiative from invading British Empire forces as they defeated the South African and British troops in the north of South Africa itself forcing the South Africans to retreat and take up defensive positions.

On the 4th February 1915 the German forces embarked on an invasion of South Africa as a pre-emptive measure to stop a further Allied invasion effort but they were thwarted at the Orange River and soon South Africa was in a position to mount an attack of its own. The Germans were defeated in two separate battles and so surrendered on 9th July 1915.

The Germans also made a number of small-scale attempts to invade the Portuguese West Africa colony, now better known as Angola but this 11 month campaign was unsuccessful and again the German forces were compelled to surrender.

Indian Allied Support and the German-Hindu Conspiracy

Though Britain had feared that there might be trouble in India during WW1, the reality was that Indians pulled together with Britain and the Empire and were a loyal, hardworking and valuable part of the Allied cause. This was partially because there was a perception that if India helped Britain then progress might be made on the question of Indian Home Rule.

The Indian army was huge and far outnumbered the British army. All in all 140,000 Indians were sent to the Western Front whilst 700,000 served in the Middle-East. Their casualty rate was relatively small as there was a reluctance to have them in front line roles in Europe but nevertheless 47,746 Indians died and 65,126 were injured during The Great War.

That being said there was an underground movement led by the Indian Ghadar party to take advantage of both most of the Indian and British army being posted overseas and with substantial German support spread a nationwide rebellion and this movement received support from both the Ottomans and Irish nationalists. A plot was formulated for the Indian army in South Asia to mutiny in February 1915 but the plan was thwarted when British intelligence infiltrated the organisation and arrested the ring-leaders. A number of small-scale mutinies did occur with one of the largest being in Singapore where 800 men mutinied, killing several dozen British soldiers before they were defeated in a week long battle.

Italy

Like Romania, Italy had been allied with the Central Powers since the 19th Century but it had secret designs on some Austrian territory and so secretly entered into a pact with France before the war. When the Austro-Hungarian Empire declared war, Italy insisted their alliance was a purely defensive one. Austria tried to buy off Italian neutrality by offering the French colony of Tunisia in North Africa but the Allies made a counter-offer of the Southern Tyrol and Austrian coastal regions. Italy belatedly declared war on the

Austro-Hungarians on 23rd May 1915 though not on Germany until the second half of 1916.

Italy had greater manpower than its opponent but the rugged mountain nature of the Austro-Italian borders made things difficult for them and furthermore, their Field Marshal Luigi Cadorna was tactically very naive. Though they took the town of Gorizia in the summer of 1916 things remained very static until the 26th October 1917 when with the Russians going out of the war, Austro-Hungary backed by Germany mounted a massive offensive which routed the Italian Army which was then forced to retreat over 60 miles.

In desperate straits, the Italian government called up every able-bodied adult male and fended off a number of Austro-Hungarian attacks in 1918 before defeating them decisively in the Battle of Vittorio Veneto. This allowed Italy to advance and occupy the Dalmatian coast which had been promised to them by the Allies just days before the war ended.

There were even military actions in the Asia-Pacific region as German colonies were attacked and subjugated primarily by Australian and New Zealand forces in Samoa and New Guinea and several small Pacific islands. A larger siege and battle took place at Tsingtao in China in October and November 1914 where 4,000 German and Chinese Colonial troops were eventually beaten by a massive 50,000 Japanese force backed by British troops.

21 ARMENIA

Much is known of the infamous genocide of European Jewry, Roma and others under Nazi Germany in World War 2 but sadly, this was not the first genocide in the 20th Century. An equally shocking event took place during WW1 when the Ottoman Empire enacted a policy of systematic genocide of Armenians in that part of their historic homeland that is now in Turkey. It is estimated that 1.5 million people were deliberately killed including other Christian minorities such as Greeks and Assyrians.

The Christian Armenians came under Muslim Ottoman rule in the 15th Century and lived both in Istanbul and in eastern Anatolia. Though allowed to practice their religion, they increasingly were treated as second class citizens. Whilst other Christian groups rebelled following Turkish attempts at reform; the 3 million Armenians stayed loyal. However, it did them little good and up to 300,000 were massacred under tacit approval of the Bloody Sultan, Abdul Hamid II. In 1909 a further 30,000 were massacred at Adana.

Following the loss of most of their European territories, the Ottomans saw Anatolia (modern day Turkey) as their final refuge and many took the view that minorities should be expelled or eliminated to ensure the stability of the homeland. Around 850,000 Muslim refugees were re-settled from Europe to Armenian homelands and they were keen to get revenge on Christian minorities, something which was encouraged by government propaganda and later revelations of military orders to massacre civilians.

When war came, many Armenians were naturally sympathetic to Russian forces who they hoped might win them their freedom. Fearful of an uprising from those armed Armenian units in the Ottoman Army, the Armenians were disbanded into labour squads.

On the 19th April 1915, Jevdet Bey arrived at the city of Van and ordered that 4,000 Armenian men be handed over under the pretext that they would be conscripted. The reality was that they were likely to be massacred, an idea made more likely by the Turk announcing he would kill every Christian man, woman and child above knee height as he had done in small villages nearby. The city of Van went under siege, defended by 1,500 Armenian riflemen who held off the Ottomans until the Russians arrived on 17th May.

It is generally assumed that this policy started on 24th April 1915 when 250 Armenian intellectuals and community leaders were arrested in Istanbul. Ottoman military forces then forced Armenians from their home and marched them hundreds of miles to the Syrian Desert without food, water or supplies. On the way there were massacres and sexual abuses regardless of age or sex.

One terrible occasion saw 5,000 Armenian villagers rounded up and burned alive, something that shocked even Turkish witnesses many of whom reported it drove them mad and that the air smelt of burning flesh for days afterwards. In the city of Trabzon, thousands of Armenians were sent out into the Black Sea on wooden boats that were then deliberately capsized with their inhabitants drowning. Others were killed by morphine injections or poison gas.

As early as May 1915, the Allies condemned the genocide that was occurring and issued a statement that those responsible would be held accountable after the war.

On 29th May the Temporary Law of Deportation was passed and soon laws were passed to appropriate abandoned property even though not all Turks agreed with it. Some such as Ottoman parliamentarian Ahmed Riza protested that the laws were unconscionable and illegal. German engineers working on train lines protested at having to work amongst such awful events. 25 Concentration-style camps were established in the Ottoman borderlines with Syria and Iraq though some were only temporary transit camps or places of mass graves.

After the war a number of Ottoman officials were taken to Malta whilst a thorough investigation was made, however they were all released after three years when Mustafa Attaturk held a number of British prisoners. One man was taken to trial in Berlin but assassinated by an Armenian group in protest at the genocide before he could be sentenced.

After the war, some survivors tried to return home but were turned back. In addition to the many deaths, the Armenians lost their wealth and much of their culture. The peace treaty at the end of WW1 allowed the formation of a small Armenian nation-state but this was almost immediately attacked by the Ottomans and soon afterwards was subsumed by Russia until they again achieved independence in 1991.

The modern state of Turkey denies that the events were genocide even though many leading nations have officially backed the use of the term. Genocide Day is remembered in

Armenia, the Armenian Diaspora and many others around the world annually on April 24th.

22 THE RUSSIAN REVOLUTION

In 1914, Russia was badly prepared for a serious war having just nine years earlier been defeated in a war with against tiny and a definitely non-European power in Japan. There was a revolution in 1905 that had shaken the Russian Empire to its core, and the Tsar was forced to concede civil rights and a parliament to the Russian people. Reforms were put in place but they were half-hearted and incomplete by the time war started however peasants eager to improve their lot rallied to their nations cause to fight against the Central Powers.

To keep the empire united a great victory was needed but early Russian hopes were immediately thwarted in The Great War. At Tannenberg and the First Battle of the Masurian Lakes, in 1914, Russia lost two entire armies of over 250,000 men.

Russia's failed advance westwards into Germany had the result of disrupting the Schlieffen Plan and possibly saved Paris from falling under the German regime but for Russia itself it was the beginning of a long retreat which saw all of Poland, Lithuania and most of Latvia in German hands by the middle of 1915.

A programme was put in place to militarise vital industrial sectors and a breakdown of the system which brought foods from the countryside to the cities meant Russia entered a serious internal crisis.

By the middle of the war things had picked up for Russia and by 1916 they had improved the supply of rifles and artillery shells to the Eastern Front. June 1916 saw a great Russian victory over Austro-Hungary with the Brusilov Offensive which resulted in the capture of Galicia and the Bukovina as well as holding off the Ottomans in the Caucasus region.

Rumours began to spread that the Tsarina Alexandra and Rasputin were German spies and despite the rumours being totally unfounded, more and more senior Russians began asking whether their 1.7 million dead and 5 million wounded was due to treason as opposed to simple stupidity and the horrors of modern warfare.

As in Britain, the out-dated strategies of the Russian generals cost countless lives, unnecessarily so in many cases and to make things worse, the Tsar and his immediate circle didn't seem to have any sympathy for the people.

After massive public demonstrations, food riots and a mutiny at the Petrograd Garrison in February 1917, Tsar Nicholas II was forced to abdicate as war continued to rage. A new and Provisional Government led by liberals and moderate socialists was proclaimed, and its leaders hoped now to pursue the war more effectively.

Tsar Nicholas and his family were put under house arrest in the Alexander Palace before later being relocated to a more remote location, supposedly for their own protection. Conditions for the Tsar were at first comfortable before things became stricter with the family being put on rations and be liable to offensive treatment from their protectors.

In April the family were moved to Yekaterinburg where the Bolsheviks wanted to put them on trial. However, the city was being threatened by the White Russians and the

Bolsheviks were worried the Tsar would be restored to power or, at least, become a figurehead of resistance. When forces from Czechoslovakia neared the city, oblivious to the fact that the Tsar was there, the Bolsheviks panicked, and the Tsar with his family were shot and also bayoneted to death on 17th July 1918.

Following the 1917 revolution, power was went to the elected Petrograd Soviet of Workers' and Soldiers' Deputies group whilst Bolshevik and Anarchist movements did their best to remove the ability of the Russian army to fight.

Russian leaders half-heartedly campaigned for a general armistice without blame or territorial transfers, something that Germany obviously would never agree too given their strong position. With their planned counter-attack for the summer of 1917 withering on the vine due to the Bolshevik convictions now held by many of the men, radical anti-war leaders including Vladimir Lenin, were ferried home from exile in Switzerland in April 1917, courtesy of the German General Staff. Such was the fear of revolt all across Europe at this time that the Germans kept Lenin locked in a train cabin, guarded at all time and forbidden to speak to anyone lest he instrument a revolt in Germany! It must be said that for some time Germany had been doing its best to create disorder in Russia and by the end of 1917 is estimated to have spent 30 million in doing so.

The summer offensive was a disaster. Peasant soldiers deserted en masse to join the revolution, and fraternisation with the enemy became common leading the way open for the Lenin and his Bolsheviks to take power in the October Revolution of 1917 without any resistance.

After taking power, the Bolsheviks promised to deliver 'Peace, Bread and Land' to the beleaguered people of Russia. With regards to the first of these, a 'Decree on Peace' (26 October 1917) was signed off by Lenin, calling upon all belligerents to end the slaughter of World War One.

It is important not to think that Lenin was a pacifist, far from it and instead he hoped to create an international civil war as he suspected Imperial powers would continue to fight and reveal their true selves to the working class people of the empires and around the world.

Realising it would allow them the chance to bring their men and resources to the Western Front, the Central Powers agreed to a peace treaty in the Polish town of Brest-Litovsk. The Russian negotiator Trotsky tried to prevaricate which simply gave the Germans the chance to make further great advances for five days as the German soldiers did not revolt as Lenin had hoped and so Russia and the Central Powers signed Treaty of Brest-Litovsk on 3rd March 1918.

It was a very one-sided and punitive treaty which effectively handed over Russian Finland, Poland, the Baltic provinces, Ukraine and Transcaucasia to the Central Powers, together with one-third of the old empire's population, one-third of its agricultural land and three-quarters of its industries.

23 THE AMERICANS ARE COMING!

When war was declared in Europe, the United States of America had no interest in joining what they labelled as the European War. American doctrine of the time was insular with regards to the old world and instead concentrated on shaping the Americas as to its own liking. Indeed a significant portion of the American public had sympathies with the Axis Powers rather than the Allies, primarily amongst Irish, German and Scandinavian settlers although generally there was an underlying sympathy in most Americans for their Anglophile cousins.

Despite the best efforts of President Woodrow Wilson to keep a policy of neutrality, a number of factors gradually led the American people to become outright hostile to the Axis forces. The rape of Belgium by the German army was well publicised with the countless deaths of civilians and ill-treatment of women and children.

On 7th May 1915, as part of its policy of submarine warfare specifically targeting Great Britain but in reality against all ships, Germany sank the Cunard liner the RMS Lusitania. Its U-boat U20 torpedoed the liner just 11 miles off the Irish coast causing the deaths of 1,198 people. It caused a worldwide controversy, not lessened by the fact that the German embassy in the United States had printed an advert warning passengers that any vessels flying the British flag or entering British waters were a possible military target.

The Royal Navy had some success tracking U-20 though couldn't stop the submarine from sinking vessels in the mid-Atlantic. The German Navy had recently cracked a British code which the Royal Navy used to telegraph civilian vessels. As such no transmissions were sent to ships in this period in case the U-Boats would be able to use them to track down Allied shipping.

Captain Turner of the Lusitania did everything possible to avoid a sinking but technology and anti-submarine techniques were in their infancy and when the Lusitania reached the southern Irish Sea, they were almost a sitting duck in a an area heavily infested with German U-Boats..

According to Maritime Law, any civilian ships targeted had to be given time to evacuate and indeed the U-20 had already followed this policy when it sank other vessels but with the Lusitania this was not the case. Germany tried to justify the sinking by claiming the Lusitania was carrying large amounts of arms and ammunitions, that it was a valid target and that as it had warned passengers of the possibility of attack, it should be absolved of any blame. However 128 Americans lost their lives and it caused outrage in America, quite aside from the hundreds of British killed in the sinking.

President Wilson came under ever increasing pressure to declare war on Germany but he was determined not to rush into armed conflict and instead urged Germany to apologise for the attack and compensate the victims of the attack as well as promising not to attack civilian ships of any flag in the future.

Germany portrayed itself to America as a victim of a British policy of an illegal blockade that was starving its people and that it had the right to try and do the same to Great Britain even if it was only able to do so through submarine warfare. President Wilson didn't buy into this point of view but refused to go to war.

Opinion amongst the British public, media and politicians was almost one of disgust at the policy chosen by the American president, seemingly unaware that he was simply following American public opinion. It is said that when shells failed to explode on the Western Front that they were labelled "Wilsons". There was a feeling in Britain that America was either too prideful or too scared to go to war and this wasn't disputed by members of the American Preparedness Movement.

By 1916, more Americans began to support entering the war, if only for reasons of nationalism and trade. A German undercover agent left his briefcase on a train in the United States and it revealed all sorts of policies and secrets that were soon published in the American papers. The British, of course, had their own propaganda campaign but weren't involved in illegal subterfuge or at least if they were, weren't stupid enough to get caught like Germany. An example of British propaganda was the successful British ploy of telling America that German school children were given a day off each year to celebrate the sinking of the Lusitania. Of course it was untrue but the Americans believed it and it was always in the interest of Britain to get America to enter the wall as quickly as possible.

Despite the promise from Germany, further ships were sank with the loss of further American lives and the feeling grew in America that they should become allies of Great Britain. After their defeat at Jutland in 1916, Germany in 1917 announced a totally unrestricted policy of targeting vessels. The outrage this caused finally saw President Wilson change his policy and on April 6th 1917 the United States declared war on Germany.

For its first year, the American build-up and participation was low-key but all sides knew that if Germany didn't win before full-scale American involvement then they never would. In March 1918, Germany launched an all-out assault on the Western Front and came close to succeeding at overwhelming the Allies but it was not enough and by April 1918 1 million American soldiers had arrived and the result of the war was then unavoidable.

Even after the war, the majority of the American public believed their wartime intervention has been a mistake and an estimated 300,000 men had illegally avoided conscription all together. The U.S. Senate rejected both the Versailles Treaty and membership of the League of Nations. Laws were put in place to try and preserve neutrality in any further conflicts and it took not just the fall of France or the sight of Great Britain standing alone against Fascism but the attack on Pearl Harbour before public sympathy decided to fight again.

24 THE HUNDRED DAY OFFENSIVE

The Western Front is often categorised as being a static war with little or no progress made by either side despite major attempts costing too many lives. However, the generals on both sides did adapt to the times. More importantly advances in technology, especially the invention of the tank made things a lot more flexible during 1917 and with the imminent arrival of the Americans, Kaiser Wilhelm decided to make a big push in the spring of 1918 utilising the almost 50 additional divisions freed up by the treaty with Russia. The hope was that Germany could overwhelm the Allies before their reinforcements arrived from across the Atlantic and involved outflanking the British and defeating them before forcing France to sue for peace.

On 21st March 1918, Germany opened Operation Michael. The Germans made some major advances as the British concentrated their forces around vital areas such as the Channel Ports and Amiens leaving other areas lightly defended. The Germans made such progress that they had problems supplying their advancing army and their storm-troopers who for the sake of mobility could only carry a few days supplies and so couldn't sustain themselves resulting in the advances faltering. The Germans had captured large amounts of tactically worthless land and suffered so many casualties that it wouldn't be easy for them to hold it in the event of a counter-attack.

Using new tactics and weaponry in August 1918, the Allies began what is known as the Hundred Day Offensive when the Allies repeatedly pushed the Germans back all the way out of France. Some of the German positions had been weakened even more by the Australian tactic of "Peaceful Penetration" wherein they would raid across no-mans land and capture German outposts, taking the German soldiers prisoners. The Battle of Amiens on the 8th August involved 10 divisions of troops supported with 500 tanks. Having achieved complete surprise, the British Fourth Army broke through the German lines with tanks reaching even their rear positions. It created a 15 mile gap in the German lines south of the Somme and German General Ludendorff labelled it the "Black Day of the German Army" due to 30,000 being killed and 17,000 being taken prisoner not to mention all of the heavy equipment that was captured by the Allies. Having lost about 12 miles of territory, the Germans withdrew from many of the positions they won in the spring offensive.

Despite French urging, General Haig paused before launching another fresh offensive on 21st August with the Battle of Albert which captured the town and pushed the Germans back another 34 miles. The British widened their scope of attack as did the French and gains were made over a large area of the front. East of Amiens, the British continued the fight and along with the French pushed the Germans back to the Hindenburg Line by mid-September.

The Hindenburg Line was a long chain of German defensive fortifications and on 26th September, French General Foch launched his 'Grand Offensive' with the support of the American Expeditionary Forces. Two days later a Belgian-backed British offensive saw the Fifth Battle of Ypres take place in Flanders. Despite the deteriorating morale and conditions of the Germans, it still took until early October until the Hindenburg Line was broken.

The Battle of Cambrai saw 3 British Armies and Canadians troops utilise tanks and air-support to quickly overwhelm the Germans with relatively low losses themselves. This collapse forced the German High Command to realise that the war had to end and quickly. The Allies also realised that rather than prepare for a big push into Germany in 1919, the war could end a great deal sooner.

25 THE ARMISTICE

The Great War ended much differently than the never-say-die desperation of the Nazis in WW2. In 1918, there was no likely imminent collapse of Germany though the deprivation and starvation of many in the country was startling. Even though there were mutinies in the ranks of the French, order was generally maintained and despite the most bloody and devastating defeats, Britain maintained is discipline and low rates of mutiny or desertion. This wasn't the case for the German army where there were increased rates of surrender and desertion. This is most likely because no matter how bad things were, the British and French never had any doubts that they wouldn't lose the war but since American entry into the war this was obviously not the case to any German soldier with any sense.

It was well known that should the war continue into 1919 that the Allies would mount a massive attack with the millions of additional American soldiers that had entered the fray, it was clear that the end was coming for the Kaiser and that it would be better to try and negotiate some sort of surrender rather than be occupied.

Additionally there was widespread civil unrest within Germany itself due to the effects of the Royal Navy blockade and so Germany decided to enter into high level discussions with the Allies for 3 days. Unknown to the Allies the German delegation had been ordered to agree to any terms put before them and this is what happened on the 11th November.

Just after 5 o'clock in the morning of 11th November 1918, British, French and German officials gathered in a railway carriage to the north of Paris and signed a document which would in effect bring to an end World War 1. It took only a few minutes before news of the Armistice flashes around the world. However, the cease-fire was set at 11am that morning to make sure all soldiers on all sides would get the news and avoid any unnecessary deaths. However, that last day of the war still saw over 10,000 casualties which is actually more than on D-Day except here many of them were pointless and entirely avoidable as their commanders already new of the impending cease-fire.

Faring particularly badly on Armistice Day were the Americans. Led by General Pershing, he seemingly learnt little from the experience of their Allies, many American commanders made the most bull-headed decisions regardless of the well-being of their men or the known fact that the war was coming to an end. Some still had the enthusiasm for fighting that the British and French had long since lost and believed they had to exact maximum punishment on Germany believing the Armistice was a mistake whilst others had far less understandable reasons.

A good example of this is that case of General William Wright of the 89th American Division. Knowing that the Armistice was just hours away but learning that the nearby town of Stenay still had washing facilities he decided to take the town so that he could enjoy the next few days in relative comfort. His idiotic decision cost 365 American casualties alone.

The final British soldier to die was that of Private George Edwin Ellison, aged 40 who was a regular in the army even before the war. He was killed whilst scouting on the edge of Mons, just a short walk from where the first casualty of the war had fallen 4 years earlier. Almost a million British deaths later and just an hour or so from being told he could return home to his wife Hannah and 4 year old son James, he was shot dead. In fact, cemeteries in Mons have graves to people killed in both the first and last days of the war and by chance, both the first British soldier killed and the last are buried opposite each other just a few feet apart.

At 10.45am a French soldier by the name of Augustin Trebuchon was taking a message to his comrades that soup would be served a few minutes after peace fell when he was killed. Like many French soldiers killed on the last day, his gravestone records his death as occurring on the 10th November mostly likely to ensure that his widow would have no problems receiving a war pension.

A few minutes later, again near Mons, 25-year-old George Lawrence Price, a Canadian Private was chasing retreating soldiers through the streets. He entered a cottage from the front street as German soldiers fled through the back door, as he emerged outside he was shot and killed at 10.58am.

Perhaps most tragically of all was the case of the final death before the Armistice that of German descended American soldier Henry Gunther who was involved in a last minute charge against a German machine gun position. The Germans were well aware it was the just before the Armistice and shouted for the attack to stop and to go back but as a matter of self-preservation they were forced to open fire and shot Henry dead at 10.59am. Even his official

Divisional records state "Almost as he fell, the gunfire died away and an appalling silence prevailed."

At 11am a young German office called Tomas approached a group of Americans to inform them that they could have the house they had been defending as the German soldiers were leaving it. These Americans didn't know of the Armistice and killed the German. All these people and many more were killed whilst people in London, Paris and even New York were already celebrating.

26 AFTERMATH

The Great War had repercussions that shook the world. The Russian Revolution brought in an era of Communism that shrouded much of the world for the rest of the 20th Century and in some places such as China indeed still does. The Baltic States gained their independence at least until the Soviet Union forcefully took control and while Finland was spared this fate, it had to fight a number of wars to protect itself. Poland also gained its freedom thanks to Lenin who renounced Russia's territorial claims.

The end of WW1 saw the Ottoman Empire capital city of Istanbul occupied by the Allies. The Treaty of Sevres in 1920 provided for the dismemberment of the remaining Ottoman provinces and under British support, Greece invaded Anatolia which set off a chain of events with severe Turkish resistance leading to the establishment of Turkey by Kemal Attaturk as moderate and west-leaning Muslim Republic.

The creation of the League of Nations was a pre-cursor to the modern day United Nations and the former Ottoman possessions in the Middle-East were given mandate status with France being tasked with bring Syria and Lebanon to a self-governing status and Great Britain being tasked with doing the same for Trans-Jordan and Palestine. Saudi Arabia gained independence whilst other areas such as Iraq came more fully into the realm of the British. The small matter of The Balfour Declaration also set in course the eventual creation of the State of Israel.

The Caucus states were soon incorporated into the Soviet Union and did not regain their independence for many decades.

The Austro-Hungarian Empire was the third of the great old European empires that met its end in WW1. Many of the subject peoples became fiercely nationalist and were on the verge of creating their new nations almost before the war finished whilst states that had won their freedoms from the Ottomans in the 19th Century such as Romania took the opportunity to reclaim territory which they saw as historically being their own. Allied powers were meant to occupy the empire to oversee a smooth transition but often were unable to due to scant resources and in many cases the defacto results were simply recognised in the Treaty of Versailles. One of the main results of this however were that many large ethnic groups were separated from their homelands in new states.

Immediately after the war in Germany, Kaiser Wilhelm II was forced to abdicate and the Weimar Republic was created. With the Allies threatening to invade, on 28th June 1919 Germany was forced to sign The Versailles Treaty, which put the entire blame for the war on Germany.£6.6 billion in reparations. Additionally, the territories won in the Treaty of Brest-Litovsk were granted their independence. It was a massive amount even for the time and it prevented the country from recovering following the war. Many in Germany then and outside of Germany now saw the amount as being far too high and humiliating for the country though it is fair to say this wasn't the prevailing view back then. Additionally, the territories won in the Treaty of Brest-Litovsk were granted their independence.

Germany suffered from hyperinflation and indeed it took until 2010 before its final reparations for WW1 were made. The treaty forced Germany to reduce the size of its armed forces. Small territory transfers were made to Belgium, Denmark, Czechoslovakia and larger amount given to France but the loss of so much land to the reformed Polish state was a breeding ground of discontent in Germany and many in the country disagreed with the whole treaty even though it was less harsh than those Germany had enforced on its victims. Nevertheless an impoverished and humiliated civil society was a fertile breeding ground for Adolf Hitler and his Nazi movement which argued the treaty had gone too far.

In the United States, the controversial Espionage Act of 1917 stayed on the statute books for decades and there were mixed feelings of how and where to help a devastated Europe with many being of the opinion that only those Allied states that had been hit by the war should be assisted. However, the USA soon entered The Great Depression after-which it decreased investment in Europe with its economic uncertainty spreading to the old world.

France annexed the Alsace-Lorraine region from Germany as it wanted to protect itself from future German aggression. The Treaty of Versailles oversaw reparations but Field Marshal Foch believed that as the state of Germany came through things intact that there was no real peace but merely a 20 year Armistice which would turn out to be eerily correct prediction. For the longer term, the important fact is that France had relied heavily on its colonial forces and they returned back to North Africa, Indochina and Senegal only to be treated as the second class citizen they had been before the war. This led to increased unhappiness and the kernel of independence movements around the world.

Italy had been promised various German, Austro-Hungarian and Ottoman territories and though they received some, many Italians felt humiliated and the scene was set for the country to become Facist under Mussolini. China too felt short changed as it was a nominal ally but its requests for German colonies to be returned was ignored and instead these were granted to Japan, this was a key turning point for Chinese nationalism.

More than any other period, the First World War shaped modern Britain. It went from the largest overseas investor to one of the biggest debtors. The Dominion nations including Canada, Australia and New Zealand felt more confidence going forward with a new national identity and became less subservient towards London whilst nations such as India and Nigeria began to sense there was an opportunity for independence. Just as importantly, the war had stopped Britain from reforming its rule in Ireland leading to radicals to gain control and shortly afterwards the Irish Free State was born.

World War One led to universal suffrage for women in Britain and Germany, and there were huge advancements in technology and medical practices due to the necessities of war. The experiences of the war led to a 'Lost Generation' across Europe. Across Britain so many men had died that not only did women gain increased access to the workplace but there were almost 2 million unable to marry as there weren't enough men. It was the end of a long era of peace and the optimism of Britannia was now broken. Whereas those in Germany, Russia and the new European states had both new ideologies and new nations to console themselves, the sense of loss and despair in Britain at that time is impossible to overstate and in a sense is still present with us today.

Many around the world thought that Germany had not been properly pacified and in fact had emerged in quite a strong position with Austro-Hungary splitting into small states and Russian borders moving eastwards. Some in Britain believed that Germany should have been split back into the individual states that it had historically been rather than leaving it the predominant state in mainland Europe.

If the death and destruction of the war itself wasn't bad enough then the world was immediately struck by a Flu pandemic which killed up to 100 million people across the globe, an event which many historians believe was partly due to the deprivations and poverty caused by the war itself.

Many of the WW1 battlefields are still evident today, some with a little imagination required for visitors and others with their trenches and even barbed wire still intact. Even a century later farmer's still plough up munitions on a daily basis with some houses having their walls built out of stacked up artillery shells. The author has himself found numerous shell casings, bullets, shrapnel and barbed wire. What no-one sees but no-one can forget are the millions of bodies hidden under the soil outside of the official graves.

The debate goes on as to whether Britain was right to enter The Great War and it is hard to imagine that effects on Britain and the world at large would have been worse if the U.K had stayed on the sidelines. It is quite possible that France would have quickly fallen or at least been forced to sue for peace leading to a peaceful Europe. However, it would have been a Europe ruled by a cruel and vicious regime that in most ways was no different than that which Britain again stepped forward to confront just 21 years later.

27 REMEMBERING THE GREAT WAR

After 100 years, possibly the most obvious sign of WW1 these days are the War Memorials. There are WW1 memorials scattered around the world and particularly in and around the battlefield sights of northern Europe. Particularly in the British Isles, you don't have to go far to find war memorials as they can be found in almost every village, every town and city, almost every church.

In fact only 53 parishes in all of England, Scotland, Wales and Ireland were fortunate enough for all their soldiers to return after the war. Out of the tens of thousands of settlements in our islands it is almost unimaginable that there were only 53 Thankful or Blessed villages. Of these 13 became Doubly Thankful as they lost no soldiers in WW2 either.

The issue of war memorials and Allied graves came to the attention of Mr. Fabian Ware who initially created a body under the auspices of The Red Cross to document and mark the graves of fallen soldiers. Ware was too old to fight in the army and so travelled to France in 1914 to see how he could help and by 1915 had received official recognition from the Imperial War Office and by the middle of 1916 had already recorded over 50,000 Allied graves.

The Imperial War Graves Commission which today is better known as The Commonwealth War Graves Commission became responsible for war memorials and graves of Allied soldiers in WW1 and later conflicts and is jointly funded by the United Kingdom, India, Australia, New Zealand, Canada and South Africa.

All of the war dead are commemorated either on a gravestone at their burial site or on a memorial, and all are honoured and remembered equally irrelevant of their race, religion, rank or civilian background. This in itself is quite a departure from earlier conflicts in which only officers of aristocratic backgrounds were immortalised whilst their many men were generally left forgotten.

In France, many of the church graveyards began to fill up with the war dead and so Fabian Ware petitioned the French government to purchase land and issue it to the United Kingdom in perpetuity and allow Britain to maintain them as desired so long as they were accessible by public roads and not too close to towns and villages. A similar agreement was also reached with Belgium.

Even before the war ended the commission was inundated by requests for photographs of graves from relatives of fallen soldiers which became an increasingly time-consuming task. Soon the Commission undertook responsibility for more distant theatres of war including Greece, Egypt and Mesopotamia, modern day Iraq.

As reports of the grave registration work became public, the Commission began to receive letters of enquiry and requests for photographs of graves from relatives of deceased soldiers, and by 1917 seventeen-thousand photographs had been dispatched to relatives. In March 1915, the Commission, with the support of the Red Cross, began to dispatch photographic prints and cemetery location information in answer to the requests. The Graves Registration Commission became the Directorate of Graves

Registration and Enquiries in the spring of 1916 in recognition of the fact that the scope of work began to extend beyond simple grave registration and began to include responding to enquiries from relatives of those killed. The directorate's work was also extended beyond the Western Front and into other theatres of war, with units deployed in Greece, Egypt and Mesopotamia, modern day Iraq.

For a while consideration was given to repatriating the bodies of dead soldiers but the logistics of dealing with such a large number, combined with a feeling that the fallen were part of a brotherhood, resulted in plans to create permanent cemeteries and monuments in and around the battlefields. Some of the most renowned architects of the time submitted designs and the author Rudyard Kipling was given responsibility for the wording on both gravestones and memorials.

In 1920, the cemetery at Forceville became the template for all that would follow with the distinctive headstones in a walled cemetery in an English garden. Cemeteries with more than 40 graves were furnished with Cross of Sacrifice and larger cemeteries a shelter and those 1,000 graves contain a Stone of Remembrance with the inscription "Their Name Liveth for Evermore".

By 1927, when the majority of construction had been completed, over 500 cemeteries had been built, with 400,000 headstones, a thousand Crosses of Sacrifice, and 400 Stones of Remembrance. However, the Commission was also tasked with honouring the hundreds of thousands of soldiers with no known grave.

Reginald Blomfield's Menin Gate was the first memorial to the missing located in Europe to be completed, and was unveiled on 24 July 1927. Sadly it was found to have insufficient space to contain all the names of the missing as originally planned and 34,984 names of the missing were instead inscribed on Herbert Baker's Tyne Cot Memorial to the Missing. Other memorials followed including the Helles Memorial in Gallipoli designed by John James Burnet; the Thiepval Memorial on The Somme, which is the largest Commonwealth war memorial and the Arras Memorial designed by Edwin Lutyens; and the Basra Memorial in Iraq designed by Edward Prioleau Warren. The Dominions and India also erected memorials on which they commemorated their missing: the Neuve-Chapelle Memorial for the forces of India, the Vimy Memorial by Canada, the Villers-Bretonneux Memorial by Australia, the Delville Wood Memorial by South Africa and the Beaumont-Hamel Memorial by Newfoundland. Incredibly the stonemasons were still applying the finishing touches on the Menin Gate when Germany again invaded Belgium in 1940.

Commonwealth cemeteries all share the same characteristics which make them distinctive from cemeteries of other nations. Usually, there is a small register in the wall or shelter with a history of the cemetery and an inventory of the graves contained therein and the cemeteries have a Christian feeling with obvious links to the soldiers self-sacrifice.

A typical cemetery is surrounded by a low wall or hedge and with a wrought-iron gate entrance. For cemeteries in France and Belgium, a land tablet near the entrance or along a wall identifies the cemetery grounds as having been provided by the French or Belgian governments. All but the smallest cemeteries contain a register with an inventory of the burials, a plan of the plots and rows, and a basic history of the cemetery.

Cemeteries in Western Europe have grass covered pathways with small bushes or flowers planted at the base of each headstone. They are carefully chosen for their low height and ability to stop rain from splashing soil onto the headstone itself. In drier climates, indigenous plants are used throughout the cemetery as is the case for those in tropical climes.

Every grave is marked with a headstone. Each headstone contains the national emblem or regimental badge, rank, name, unit, date of death and age of each casualty inscribed above an appropriate religious symbol and a more personal dedication chosen by relatives. The headstones use a standard upper case lettering designed by MacDonald Gill. Individual graves are arranged, where possible, in straight rows and marked by uniform headstones, the vast majority of which are made of Portland stone. The original headstone dimensions were 76 cm tall, 38 cm wide, and 7.6 cm thick.

Most headstones are inscribed with a cross though depending on the faith of the soldier other symbols such as the Star of David are used. In the case of burials of Victoria Cross recipients, the regimental badge is replaced by the Victoria Cross emblem. Sometimes soldiers employed a pseudonym because they were too young to serve or were sought by the police and in these cases their second name is shown along with the notation "served as".

Many headstones are for unidentified casualties; they consequently bear only what could be discovered from the body. In these cases there is an epitaph stating "A Soldier of the Great War known unto God". Some headstones contain the text "believed to be buried in this cemetery" when they are believed to be buried in the cemetery but the exact location of the grave within the cemetery is not known. In some cases soldiers were buried not in individual graves, but collective graves and distinguishing one body from another was not possible, and thus one headstone might cover numerous dead. The headstones do not denote any specific details of the death except for its date.

The Commission is responsible for the commemoration of 1.7 million deceased Commonwealth military service members in 153 countries. Since its inception, the Commission has constructed approximately 2,500 war cemeteries and numerous memorials. The Commission is currently responsible for the care of war dead at over 23,000 separate burial sites and the maintenance of more than 200 memorials worldwide. In addition to commemorating Commonwealth military service members, the Commission maintains, under an arrangement with applicable governments, over 40,000 non-Commonwealth war graves and over 25,000 non-war military and civilian graves.

For those unable to visit the war graves overseas and in recognition of all those who died but whose bodies are unrecovered are a number of Tombs of Unknown Soldiers in Serbia, Greece, Romania, Italy, France, the United States, the Commonwealth nations of Australia, Canada, India and the Tomb of the Unknown Warrior near the entrance of Westminster Abbey in London.

Those who fought and died in The Great War are remembered in many countries around the world on Armistice Day, sometimes known as Remembrance Day or

Poppy Day. Services are held in distant cemeteries, tiny villages and magnificent cathedrals with the lead being taken by the National Service of Remembrance led by the Queen at The Cenotaph in London and attended by the Ambassadors and Commissioners of The Commonwealth which sees the city comes to a half as the chimes of Big Ben echo through the still air for two minutes silence.

At the going down of the sun and in the morning,

We will remember them.

28 MAPS AND PHOTOGRAPHS

Here are a collection of maps and photos relating to some of the major events and figures referenced in this book. The author also includes a few of his personal photos

The nine sovereigns of Europe meet in London just years before WW1.

Memorial to one of the Zeppelin bombing raids

Albatross DIII planes, with the Red Barons third from the front.

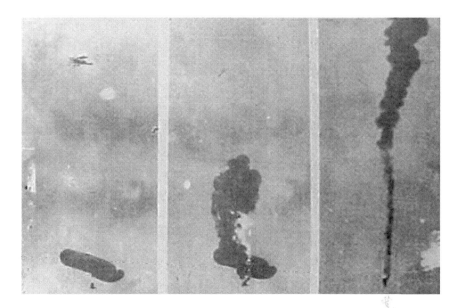

A bombed German observation balloon

HMS Iron Duke at the Battle of Jutland

Perhaps the most iconic recruitment poster of all time.

Lawrence of Arabia in Bedouin dress.

Over the top at the Battle of the Somme

Gavrillio Princip – the man whose actions were the excuse for WW1.

The Camel Corps at Bathsheeba

Manfred Von Richthoffen – The Red Baron

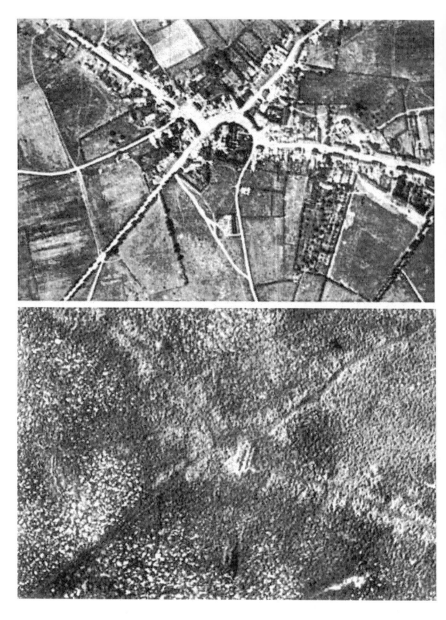

Paschendaele – Before and After.

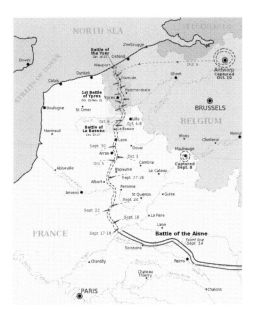

The Race to the Sea.

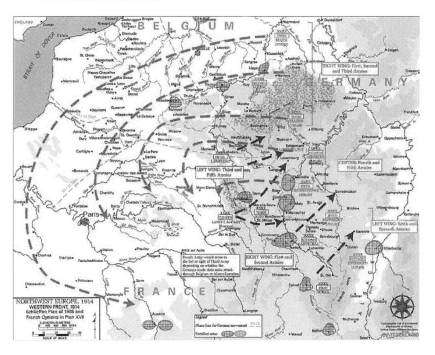

The Schieffen Plan – The German initial attacks on the Western Front

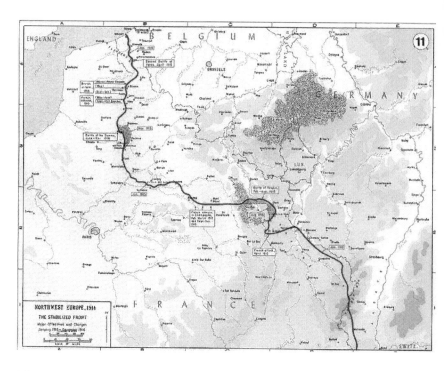

The Western Front in 1915-1916

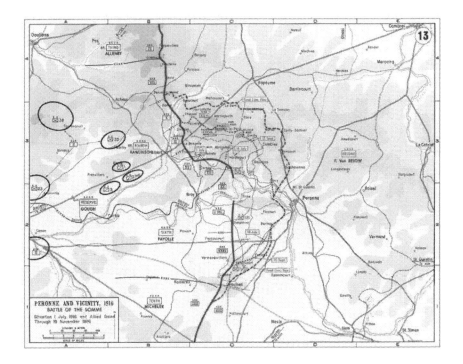

The Battle of The Somme

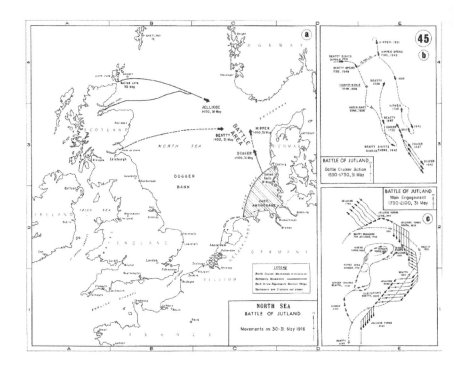

The Battle of Jutland

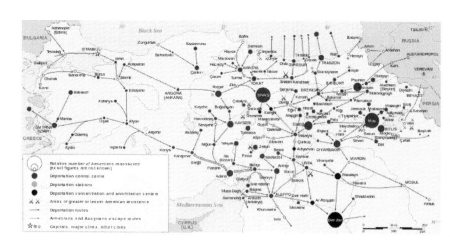

Map of Armenian Genocide locations by Semhur.

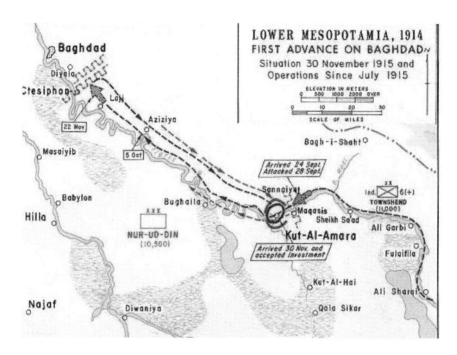

The ill-conceived British campaign in Iraq against the Ottomans.

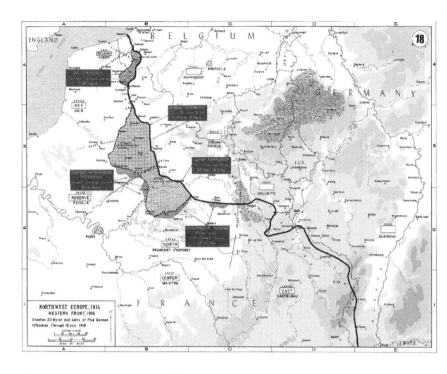

German offensives in the spring of 1918.

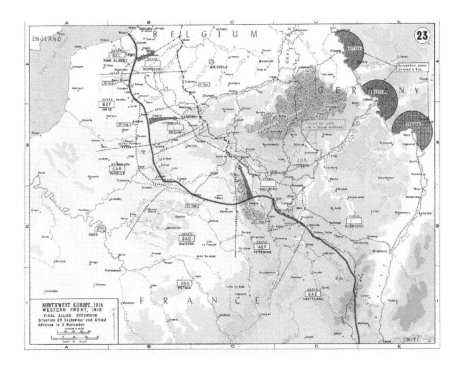

The front lines on Armistice Day.

Thiepval Memorial, the largest war memorial in the world.

The authors Great Grandfather, Private Ernest Heard S/N 24500 of The Loyal North Lancashire Regiment who died in Mesopotamia on 25th January 1917 and who is buried in Amara, Iraq.Ernest Heard with his wife Annie and son Harold.

The Authors cousin thrice removed, Serjent Reuel Dunn S/N 6396 of the Royal Flying Corp who was shot down by the Red Baron on 2nd April 1917 and is buried in the Cabaret-Rouge British Cemetery, Souchez, France

Newspaper report on Serjent Dunn's deadly battle with the Red Baron. We're very proud of him as we are off all our family members listed here and those we have no records of.

James Arthur Heard II whose father left Lancashire, England for a new life in the United States. Photographed here in the uniform of the American army.

William and Gwen Cusak – another of the authors Great Grandparents.

Enlistment form one of Robert William Liddell

Enlistment Form 2 of Robert William Liddell

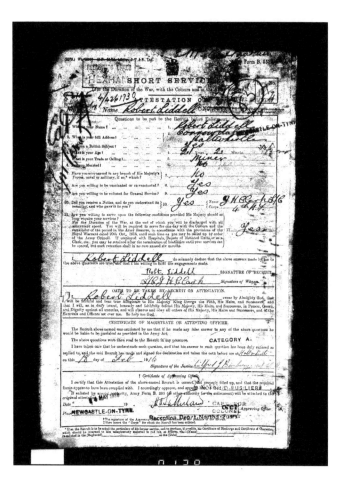

Enlistment form 3 of Robert William Liddell

In Memory of
Corporal

G H Liddell

315010, 12th/13th Bn., Northumberland Fusiliers who died on 22 August 1918

Remembered with Honour
Connaught Cemetery, Thiepval

Commemorated in perpetuity by
the Commonwealth War Graves Commission

Typical CWGC memorial page, this for my Great Great
Uncle, George Hardy Liddell who died not so far away from
Reuel Dunn.

ABOUT THE AUTHOR

Stephen Liddell is a young writer and historian who with both a BA Hons and Masters from SOAS, London University. He has visited the WW1 and WW2 battlefields extensively in northern and eastern Europe as well as also visiting the Middle-East battlefields of Lawrence of Arabia and others during multiple trips to Egypt and Jordan.

Stephen is married to Emilia and when not writing runs Ye Olde England Tours, an independent cultural tour company specialising in private tours around London and southern England.

Stephen writes regularly for various publications as well as his own website www.stephenliddell.co.uk   His early works include a humorous travelogue, 'Planes, Trains and Sinking Boats', an Amazon #1 section best seller 'How to Get Rich Using Airbnb' as well as the historical fiction trilogy 'The Promise', 'The Messenger' and 'Forever and Until'.

Readers who enjoyed this book may also enjoy 'In The Footsteps of Heroes' a photo tour of the Western Front.

In 2015 Stephen published a short horror story entitled 'The Silence Fell' and 'Very Sad Poetry', a collection of poems whilst 2016 saw the release of V1 Vixen, a pulp noir vigilante thriller.

If you have any questions or opinions please email Stephenliddell@gmail.com

10449 PARISHES

Printed in Great Britain
by Amazon